E S T A T E   P U B L

C000269593

FAREHAM - GO⎵. ⎵...

SARISBURY · WARSASH · TITCHFIELD
PORTCHESTER · STUBBINGTON · LEE-ON-SOLENT

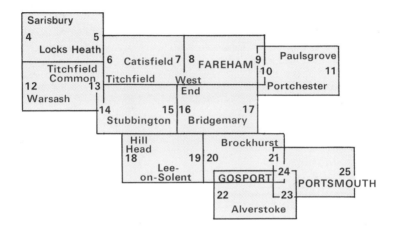

Sarisbury

4   5
Locks Heath
           6   Catisfield 7 8 FAREHAM 9 Paulsgrove
Titchfield   10   11
Common Titchfield   West   Portchester
12   13   End
Warsash
        14   15 16   17
        Stubbington Bridgemary

        Hill   Brockhurst
        Head
        18   19 20   21
           Lee-   24   25
           on-Solent   GOSPORT   PORTSMOUTH
                       22   23
                       Alverstoke

ROAD MAP   pages 2–3
INDEX TO STREETS page 26

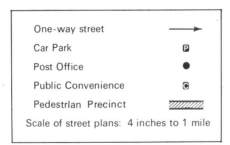

One-way street	⟶
Car Park	Ⓟ
Post Office	●
Public Convenience	Ⓒ
Pedestrian Precinct	▨

Scale of street plans: 4 inches to 1 mile

Street plans prepared and published by ESTATE PUBLICATIONS,
Bridewell House Tenterden Kent and based upon the ORDNANCE
SURVEY maps with the sanction of the controller of H.M Stationery Office

The publishers acknowledge the co-operation of Fareham and Gosport
District Councils in the preparation of these maps.

© Estate Publications 070   Crown copyright reserved

ISBN 0 86084

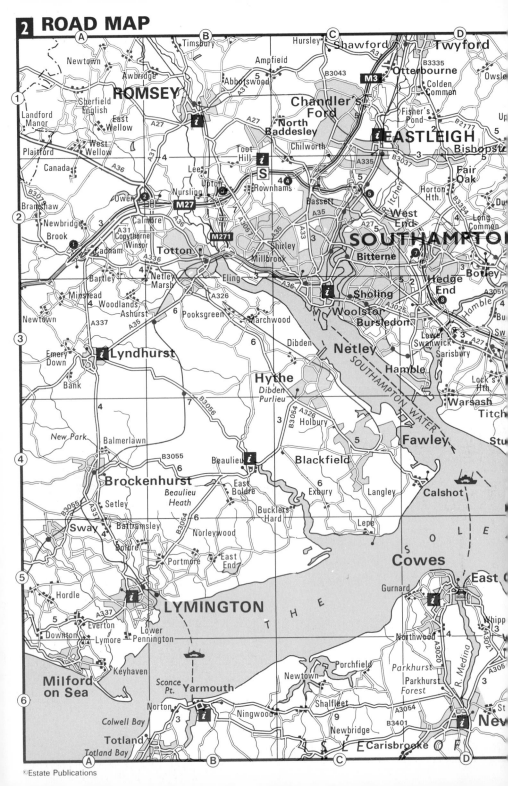

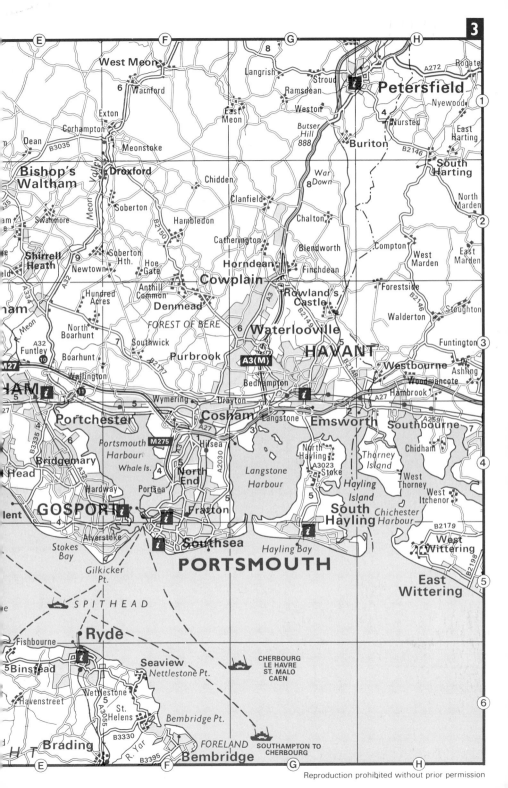

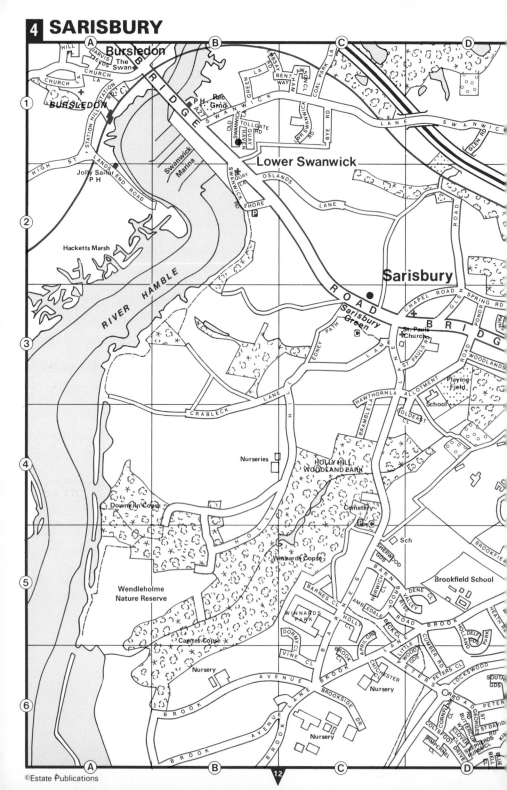

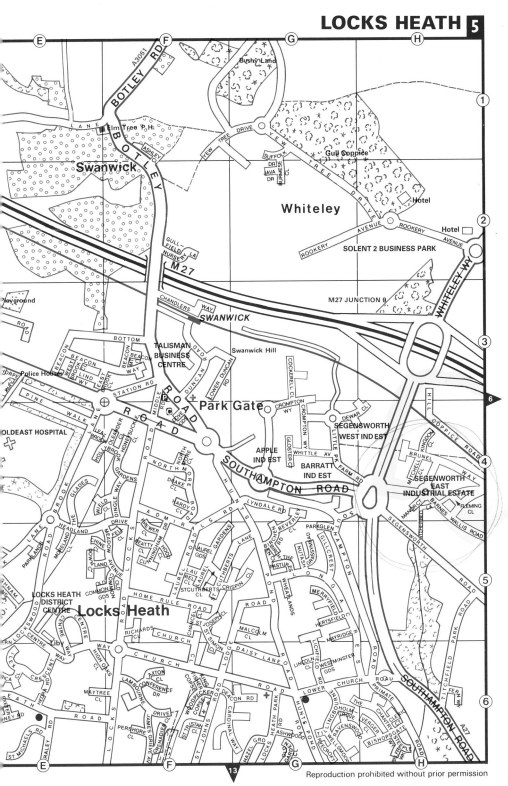

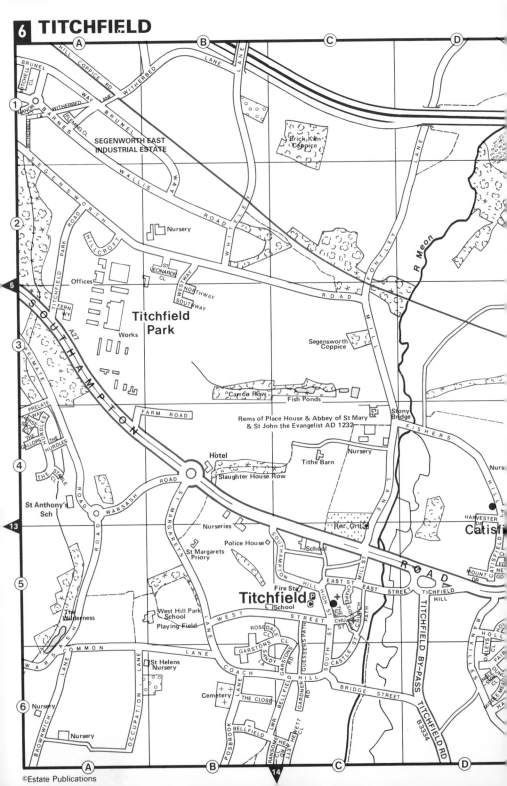

©Estate Publications

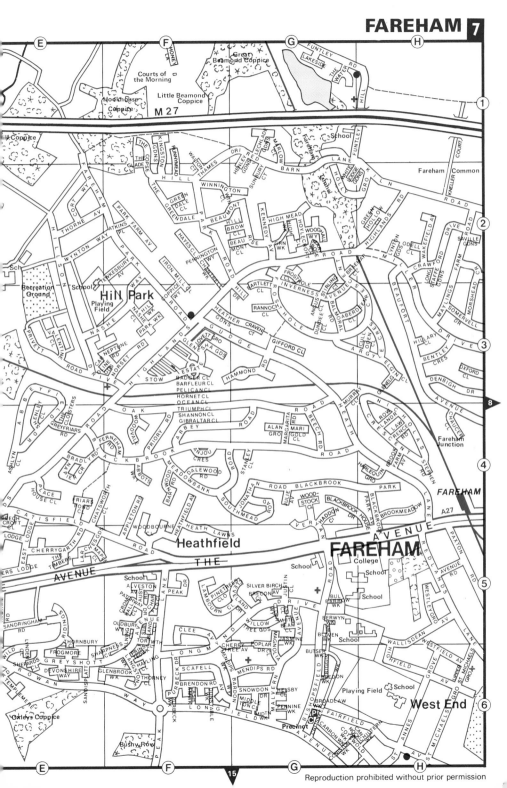

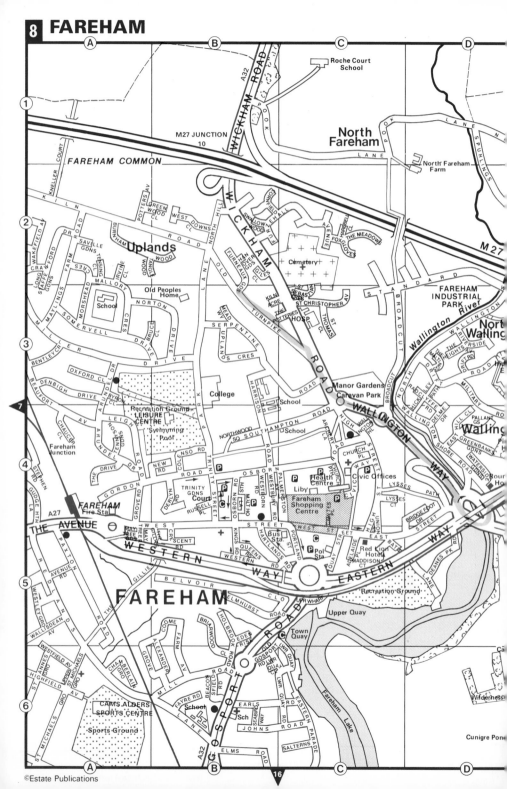

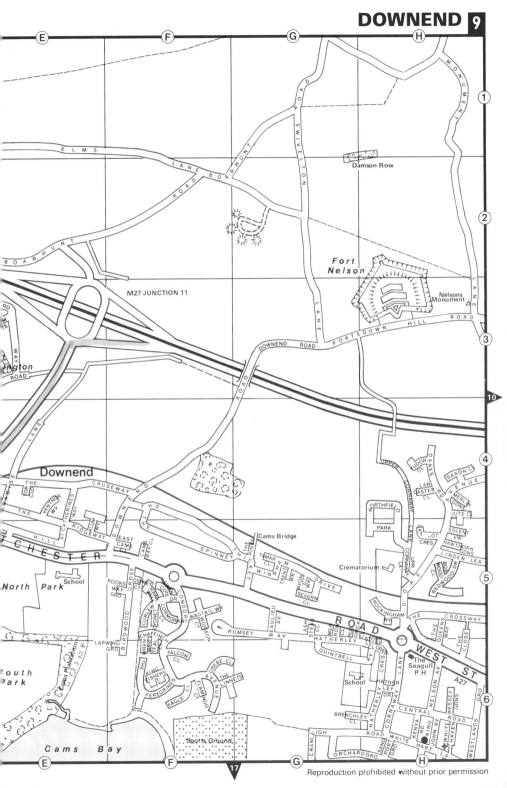

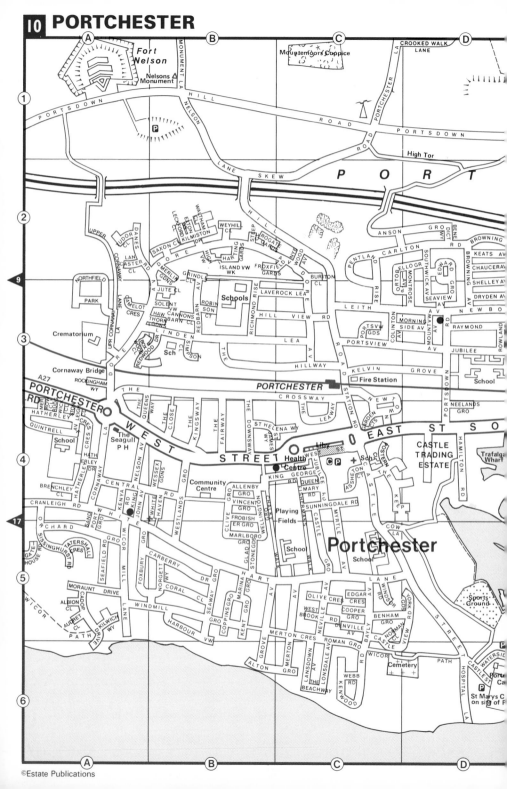

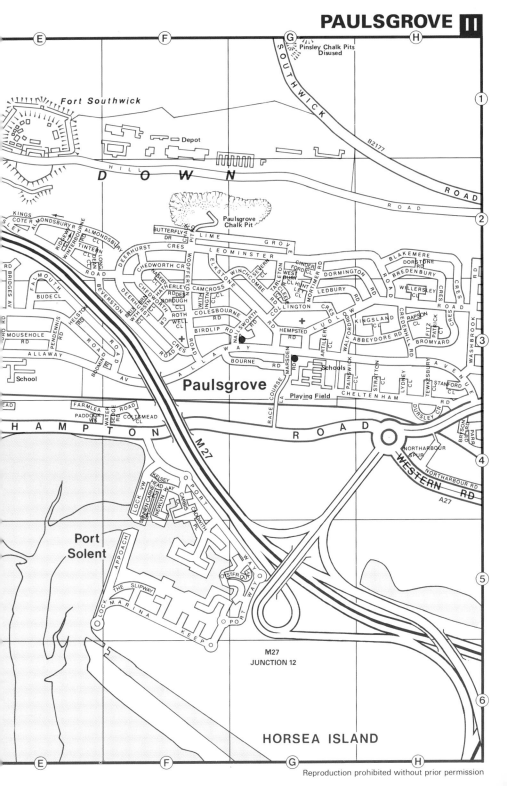

Port
Solent

Paulsgrove

HORSEA ISLAND

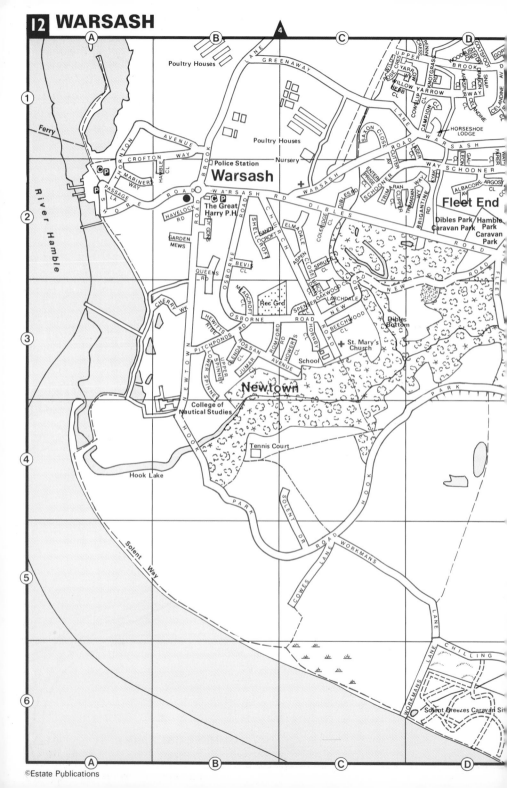

©Estate Publications

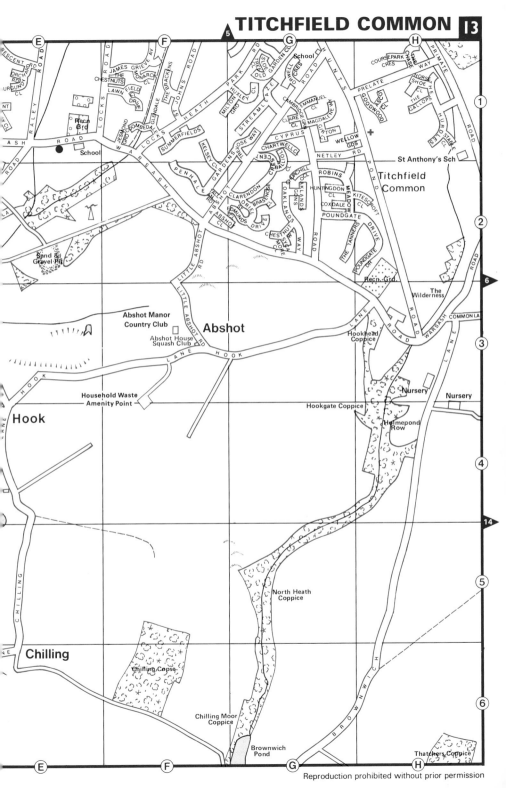

Titchfield
Common

St Anthony's Sch

Abshot Manor
Country Club

Abshot House
Squash Club

Abshot

Household Waste
Amenity Point

Hook

Hookhead
Coppice

Hookgate Coppice

Nursery

Nursery

Helmepond
Row

North Heath
Coppice

Chilling

Chilling Copse

Chilling Moor
Coppice

Brownwich
Pond

Thatchers Coppice

The
Wilderness

Recn. Grd.

Sand &
Gravel Pit

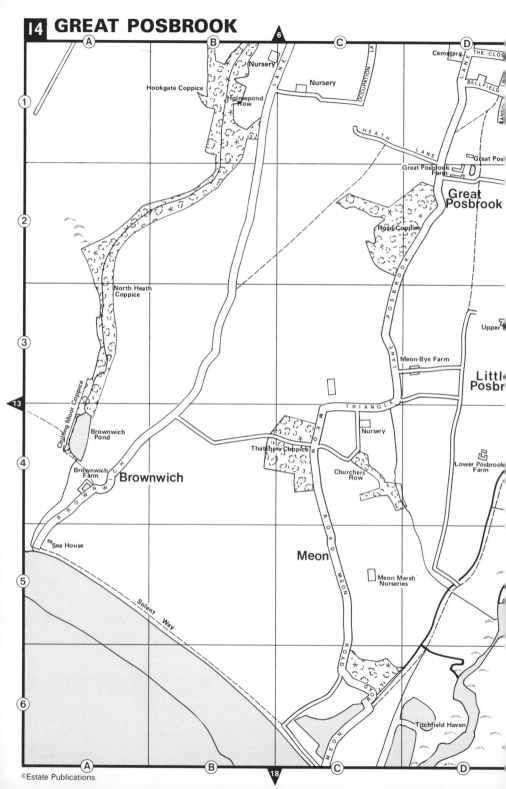

Nursery

Hookgate Coppice

Holmepond Row

Nursery

OCCUPATION LA

Cemetery

THE CLOS

LANE

BELLFIELD

HEATH LANE

Great Pos

Great Posbrook Farm

Great Posbrook

Road Coppice

POSBROOK LANE

North Heath Coppice

Upper

Meon-Bye Farm

Chilling Moor Coppice

13

Brownwich Pond

TRIANGLE

Little Posbr

MEON

Nursery

Thatchers Coppice

Brownwich Farm

Brownwich

Churchers Row

Lower Posbrook Farm

BROWNWICH

Sea House

ROAD MEON

Meon

Meon Marsh Nurseries

Solent Way

MEON ROAD

Titchfield Haven

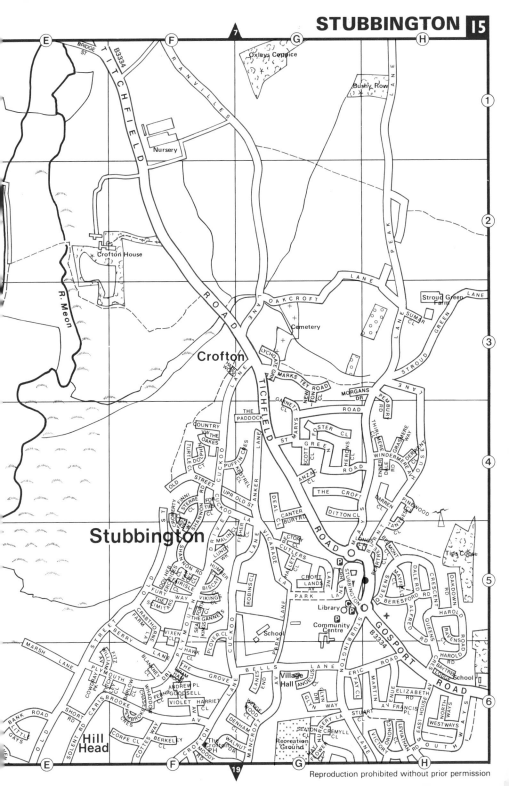

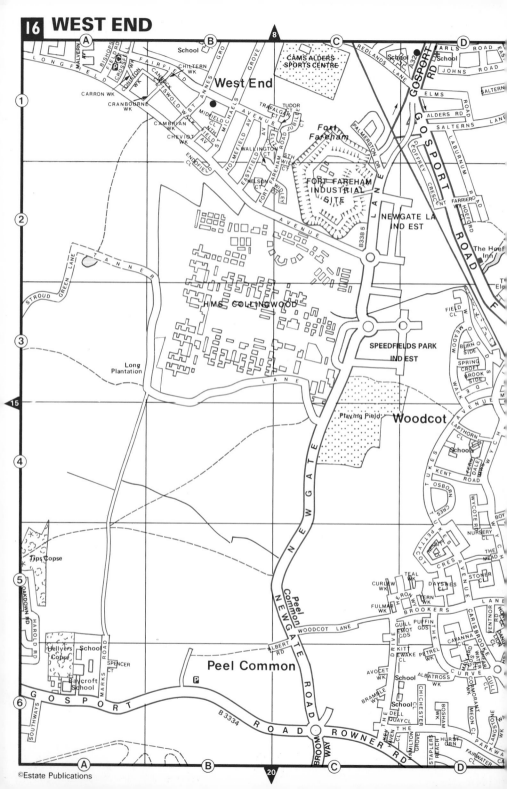

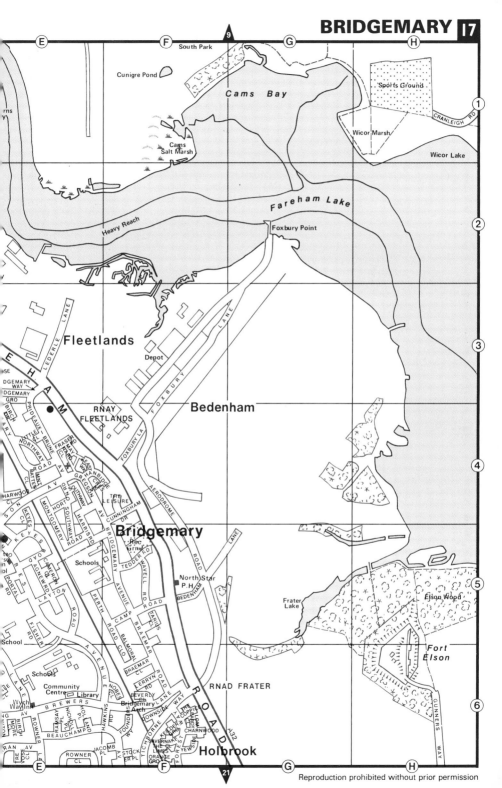

E F South Park G H

Cunigre Pond

Cams Bay

Sports Ground

Wicor Marsh

CRANLEIGH RD

1

rns

Cams
Salt Marsh

Wicor Lake

Fareham Lake

Heavy Reach

Foxbury Point

2

Fleetlands

Depot

3

FOXBURY LANE

LEDERLE LANE

SE

DGEMARY
WAY
DGEMARY
GRO

RNAY
FLEETLANDS

Bedenham

FOXBURY LA

AERODROME ROAD LANE

H
E
A
M

BIRCH

PAD PAUL BRUNE

LITTLE CL

FRASER RD

WHANBIDGE CL

GREGSON AV

NORTHWAY

BATTEN

THE
LEISURE

CUNNINGHAM DR

4

HARWOOD

CLON

KEYES

HORT CL

SOUTHWAY

HARRISD AV

BRIDGEMARY AV

Bridgemary

Rec
Grd

BALMORAL ROAD

MONTGOMERY

CAMERON

AGNEW RD

Schools

TEDDER RD

WAVELL ROAD

FARIS
ROAD

LANE

North Star
P.H.

Frater
Lake

Elson Wood

5

PORTAL RD

LAYTON

PERTH ROAD

AVENUE

CAMP ROAD

BRAEMAR CL

BEDENHAM

Fort
Elson

School

FISHER

BALMORAL
CL

BRAEMAR
CL

LERRYN RD

GUNNERS WAY

Schools

Community
Centre

Library

BREWERS

NOBES AV

BEVERLY
CL

Bridgemary Arch

RNAD FRATER

ROAD

A32

Wych Way

AV

BIRCH

ROWNER

HAWKINS

NICHOLL

HASLAR

TICHBORNE WAY

TOWNSIDE WAY

THE COPSE

SAVERNAKE

BEAUCHAMP

ROWNER
CL

JACOMB
PL

ORANGE
GRO

STOCKER PL

TICHFORNE

FORREST

LIMES

CHARNWOOD

YEWS

Holbrook

E F G H

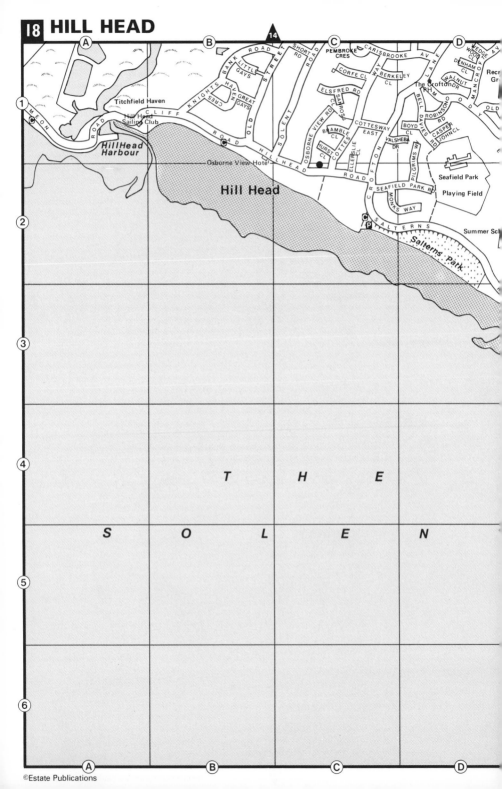

14

Titchfield Haven

Hill Head Sailing Club

CLIFF

HillHead Harbour

MEON

ROAD

Osborne View Hotel

Hill Head

BANK

KNIGHTS CRES

HAVEN

LITTLE GAYS

GREAT GAYS

STREET

ROAD

OLD

HILLHEAD

ROAD

SHORT RD

SOLENT RD

OSBORNE VIEW RD

PEMBROKE CRES

CARISBROOKE

CORFE CL

BERKELEY CL

ELSFRED RD

SANROSS

BRAMBLE CL

COTTESWAY EAST

HURST COTTES

ELLERSLIE

WAY

BELL RD

ROBINSON RD

BOYD DAVIES RD

CASPER

JOHN CL

VALSHEBA DR

The Crofton RH M

WALNUT

DENHAM CL

MANCR RD

OLD

CROFTON

ROAD

SEAFIELD PARK RD

MONKS WAY

PILGRIMS WY

Seafield Park

Playing Field

P

SALTERNS

Salterns Park

Summer Sch

T   H   E

S   O   L   E   N

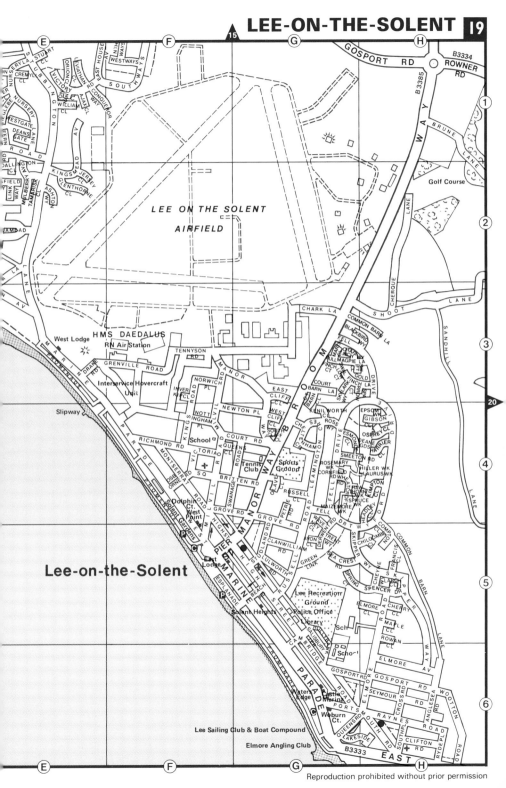

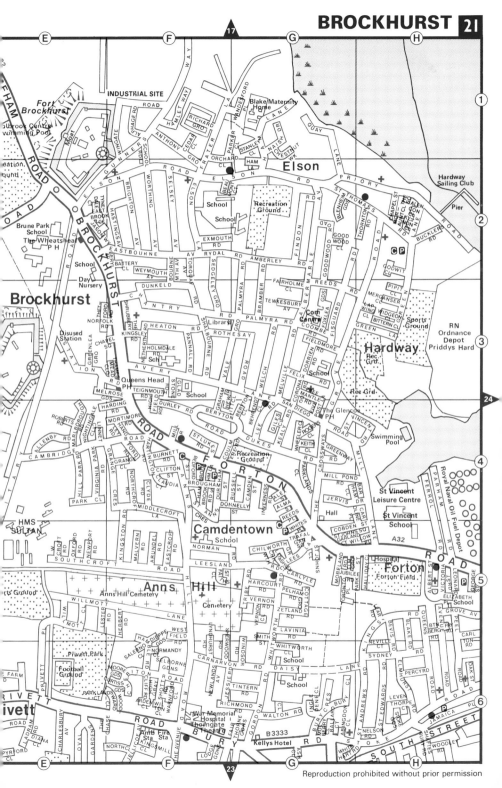

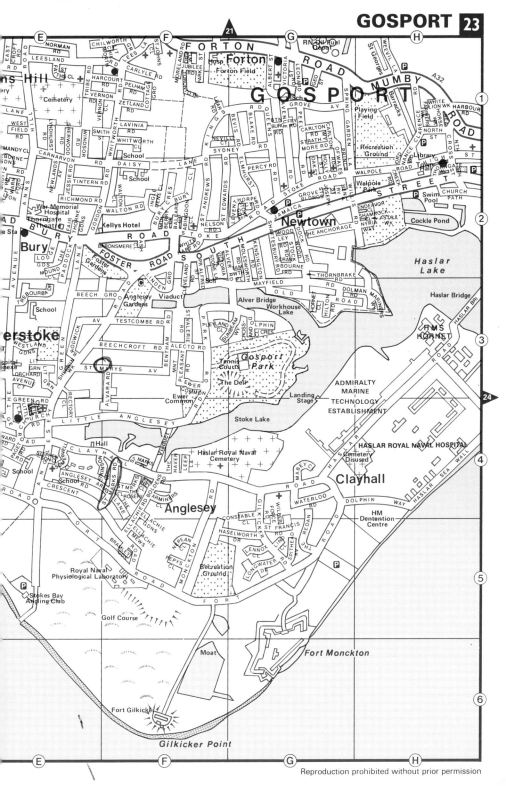

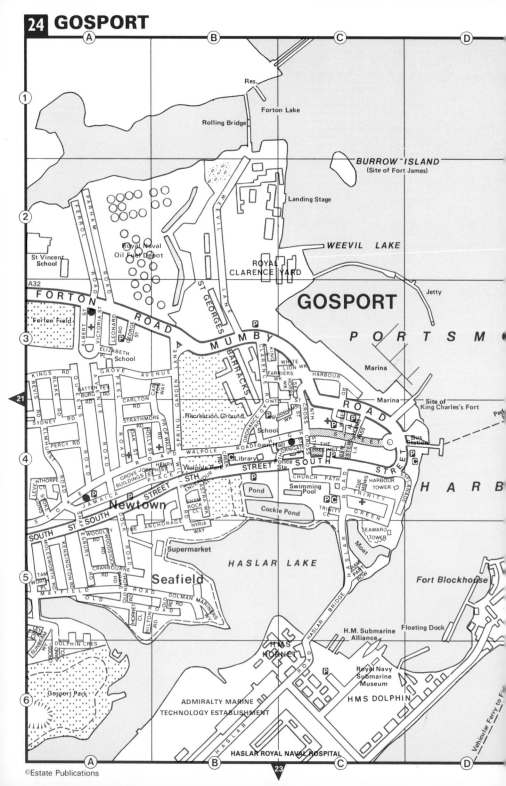

INDEX TO STREETS

The Index includes some names for which there is insufficient space on the maps. These names are preceded by an * and are followed by the nearest adjoining thoroughfare.

Abbey Rd	7 F4
Abbeydore Rd	11 H3
Abbeyfield Dri	7 E4
Abbots Way	7 F4
A'Becket Ct	25 F5
Aberdeen Clo	7 G3
Abingdon Clo	23 F2
Abshot Clo	13 F2
Abshot Rd	13 F2
Acorn Clo	20 D1
Actaeon Rd	25 E4
Addison Rd	5 E3
Adelaide Pl	8 C5
Admirals Rd	5 F4
Admirals Walk, Portsea	25 E2
Admirals Walk, Privett	22 D2
Admiralty Rd	25 F2
Aerodrome Rd	17 F4
Agnew Rd	17 E5
Ajax Way	19 E1
Alan Gro	7 G4
Albacore Av	12 D2
Albatross Walk	16 D6
Albemarle Av	21 G3
Albert Rd	16 C6
Albert St	23 G1
Albion Clo	10 A5
Aldemoor Rd	20 D3
Alder La	20 D5
Alders Rd	16 D1
Aldrich Rd	25 F1
Alecto Rd	23 F3
Alencon Clo	21 H2
Alex Rose La	25 H3
Alex St	21 G4
Alexander Gro	8 B6
Alfred Rd, Portsmouth	25 G2
Alfred Rd, Stubbington	15 H5
Allaway Av	11 E3
Allenby Gro	10 B4
Allenby Rd	21 E4
Alliance Clo	20 D2
Allotment Rd	4 D3
Alma St	21 G4
Almondsbury Clo	11 E2
Almondsbury Rd	11 E2
Almondside	20 D1
Alphage Rd	21 F1
Alton Gro	10 B6
Alum Way	9 E5
Alvara Rd	23 F3
Alver Rd	23 F2
Alvercliffe Dri	22 D4
Alveston Av	7 F5
Amberley Rd	21 G2
Ambledale	4 C5
Amersham Clo	22 C2P
Anchor Gate Rd	25 F2
Anchor La	25 E2
Andrew Bell St	25 H1
Andrew Pl	15 F6
Angelus Clo	15 G6
Anglesea Rd, Alverstoke	23 E4
Anglesea Rd, Lee-on-the-Solent	19 H6
Anglesea Rd, Portsmouth	25 G3
Anglesea Rd, Rowner	20 A6
Anglesey Arms Rd	23 E4
Angus Clo	7 G3
Anjou Cres	7 F4
Anker La	15 G4
Anker Wyke	20 B1
Anns Hill Rd	21 F4
Anson Clo	20 D5
Anson Gro	10 C2
Anthony Gro	21 F1
Anzac Clo	15 G4
Appleton Rd	7 F5
April Gro	4 C6
Archery La	8 C4
Arden Clo	21 F6
Argosy Clo	12 D2
Argyle Cres	7 H3
Ariadne Rd	25 F4
Arminers Clo	23 F4
Armory La	25 F4
Artillery Clo	11 G3

Arundel Dri	8 A4
Arundel Rd	21 F5
Arundel St	25 H2
Arundel Way	25 H2
Ascot Clo	13 H1
Ash Burton Rd	22 D4
Ash Clo, Fareham	7 G5
Ash Clo, Gosport	23 F2
Ashburton Rd	25 H6
Ashdown	20 D1
Ashley Clo	5 F1
Ashley Ct	21 G5
Ashlyn Clo	7 E4
Ashstead Clo	9 G5
Ashton Way	19 E2
Ashwood	5 G6
Aspen Av	12 C2
Aspen Gro	20 D1
Assheton Ct	10 C4
Astley St	25 G4
Astra Walk	24 B4
Atherstone Walk	25 H4
Atkins Pl	7 F2
Atkinson Clo	23 E4
Audret Clo	10 A6
Aust Rd	7 F5
Austerberry Way	20 D2
Avenue Ct	23 E3
Avenue Rd, Fareham	8 A5
Avenue Rd, Gosport	23 G1
Avery La	21 F3
Avocet Walk	16 C6
Avon Clo	19 G5
Avon Wk	9 G5
Ayling Clo	20 C3
Aylward St	25 F3

Badger Clo	7 F3
Ballard Ct	23 F2
Balliol Clo	13 G2
Balmoral Clo	17 F5
Balmoral Rd	7 G3
Bankside	23 E4
Bardon Way	7 G6
Barfleur Clo	7 F3
Barham Clo	21 G4
Barlow Clo	15 F6
Barn Brook Rd	4 C5
Barnes Clo	4 C5
Barnes La	4 C6
Barnes Wallis La	5 H4
Barnwood Rd	7 F4
Baronsmere	23 F5
Bartlett Clo	7 G3
Bath La	8 C5
Bath Sq	25 E5
Bathing La	25 E5
Battenberg Rd	24 A3
Battery Clo	21 F2
Battery Row	25 E5
Bay Rd	22 D3
Bayly Av	10 C5
Baytree Lodge	15 H6
Beach Rd	19 G5
Beacon Bottom	5 E3
Beacon Clo	5 F3
Beacon Mnt	5 F3
Beacon Way	5 E3
Beaconsfield Rd	8 B6
Beatty Clo	5 F5
Beatty Rd	23 E3
Beauchamp Av	20 C1
Beaufort Av	7 H3
Beaulieu Av	9 G5
Beaulieu Pl	16 D6
Beaumont Clo	7 G2
Beaumont Ct	21 F2
Beaumont Rise	7 F2
Beck Clo	4 C5
Beck St	25 F3
Bedenham La	17 F5
Bedford St, Brockhurst	21 F4
Bedford St, Portsmouth	25 H4
Beech Gro	23 E3
Beech Rd	7 G4
Beechcroft Clo	7 E4
Beechcroft Rd	23 F3
Beechwood Clo	12 C3
Beehive Walk	25 F4
Behrendt Clo	21 G4
Belfry Walk	5 H6
Bell Davies Rd	18 D1
Bellevue Ter	25 G6
Bellfield	6 B6
Bells La	15 G6
Belmont Clo	15 H5
Belmont Pl	25 H5

Belmont St	25 H5
Belvoir Clo	8 B5
Bemisters La	24 C4
Benbow Pl	25 F3
Benedict Way	10 D2
Beneficial St	25 F3
Benham Gro	10 C5
Bentham Rd	23 F3
Bentham Way	4 C1
Bentley Cres	7 H3
Beresford Rd	15 H5
Berkeley Clo	18 C1
*Berkeley Ct, Elmore Rd	19 H6
Berry La	15 F5
Berwyn Walk	7 G5
Beryl Av	21 F2
Beryton Clo	21 G4
Beryton Rd	21 F4
Beverley Clo	5 G5
Beverley Rd	19 E2
Beverly Clo	17 F6
Beverston Rd	11 E3
Bevis Clo	12 B2
Bevis Rd	23 G1
Biddlecombe Clo	20 C2
Biggin Walk	7 G6
Bilberry Clo	12 D1
Birch Dri	17 E4
Birchdale Clo	12 C3
Birchen Clo	5 G5
Birchen Rd	5 G5
Birchmore Clo	17 E6
Birdlip Rd	11 F3
Birdwood Gro	9 F5
Biscay Clo	15 F5
Bishop St	25 D3
Bishopsfield Rd	7 G6
Bishopsgate	5 H6
Bittern Clo	21 H3
Blackbird Way	19 H3
Blackbrook House Dri	7 G4
Blackbrook Park	7 G4
Blackbrook Park Av	7 H4
Blackbrook Rd	7 E4
Blakemere Cres	11 H2
Blake Rd	23 G1
Blankney Clo	15 F6
Blaven Walk	7 G5
Blenheim Gdns	21 G2
Blossom Sq	25 F2
Blount Rd	25 G5
Bluebell Clo	4 D6
Boarhunt Rd	9 E2
Bodmin Rd	11 E3
Boiler Rd	25 E1
Boldens Rd	23 F4
Bonfire Corner	25 F2
Bosham Walk	16 D6
Botley Rd	5 F1
Bourne Rd	11 G3
Bournemouth Av	21 F2
Boxwood Clo	10 A3
Boyd Clo	18 D1
Boyd Rd	16 D4
Bracklesham Rd	20 D2
Brading Av	17 E6
Bradly Rd	7 E4
Braemar Clo, Bridgemary	17 F6
Braemar Clo, Fareham	7 G2
Braemar Rd	17 F5
Bramber Rd	21 G3
Bramble Clo	18 C1
Bramble La	4 C4
Bramble Way	16 C6
Bramham Moor	15 F6
Bramley Gdns	23 F5
Brasenose Clo	13 G2
Braunstone Clo	11 F3
Brecon Clo	7 G5
Bredenbury Cres	11 H2
Bredon Walk	7 G6
Brenchley Clo	9 G6
Brendon Rd	7 F6
Brewer Clo	5 F5
Brewers La	17 E6
Brewers St	25 H2
Briar Clo	22 C3
Briarwood Clo	8 B5
Bridge Rd	4 A1
Bridge St	6 C6
Bridgefoot Dri	8 D4
Bridgemary Av	17 F5
Bridgemary Gro	17 E3
Bridgemary Rd	17 E3
Bridgemary Way	17 E3

Bridges Av	11 E2
Brigantine Rd	12 D2
Brighton Av	21 F2
Britain St	25 F3
Britten Rd	19 F4
Brixworth Clo	11 F3
Broad St	25 E5
Broadcut	8 C3
Broadlaw Walk	7 G6
Broadsands Dri	22 C3
Broadsands Walk	22 C3
Brockhurst Rd	21 E2
Brodwick Av	23 E3
Bromyard Cres	11 H3
Brook Av	4 B6
Brook Clo	4 C6
Brook Farm Av	7 H4
Brook La	12 B2
Brookers La	16 D5
Brookfield Gdns	4 D5
Brookmeadow	7 H4
Brookside	16 D3
Brookside Dri	4 C6
Broom Way	19 G4
Broomfield Cres	20 B3
Brougham La	21 F4
Brougham Rd	25 H4
Brougham St	21 F4
Browndown Rd	22 B3
Browning Av	10 D2
Brownwich La	14 A4
Bruce Clo	8 A3
Brune La	20 A1
Brunel Way	5 H4
Brunswick St	25 H4
*Bryony Clo, Bilberry Clo	12 D1
Bryson Rd	11 H4
Buckingham Pl	25 H2
Buckingham St	25 H2
Bucklers Rd	21 H2
Bucksey Rd	20 B2
Bude Clo	11 E3
Bulbarrow Walk	7 G6
Bullfinch Ct	19 G3
Burgundy Clo	13 E1
Buriton Clo	10 C2
Burmese Clo	5 G2
Burnaby Rd	25 G3
Burnett Rd	21 F4
Burney Rd	22 D3
Burnham Wood	8 A2
Burnhams Walk	24 C4
Burnside	16 D3
Burnt House La	15 H5
Bury Clo	23 F2
Bury Cres	23 F2
Bury Hall La	22 D3
Bury Rd	23 E2
Bush St, East	25 H5
Bush St, West	25 G5
Butchers St	25 F3
Butser Walk	7 G6
Buttercup Way	4 D6
Butterfly Dri	11 F2
Bye Rd	4 C1
Byron Clo	8 A3

Cadgwith Pl	11 F4
Cador Dri	10 A5
Caldecote Walk	25 G4
Calshot Way	20 B1
Cambrian Walk	16 B1
Cambridge Grn	13 G1
Cambridge Junction	25 F4
Cambridge Rd, Brockhurst	21 E4
Cambridge Rd, Lee-on-the-Solent	19 G5
Cambridge Rd, Portsmouth	25 G4
Camcross Clo	11 F3
Camden St	21 G4
Camelot Cres	10 A3
Cameron Clo	17 E5
Camp Rd	17 F5
Campion Clo	12 D1
Cams Hill	8 D4
Camsbay Clo	9 F5
Cannock Walk	7 G6
Cannons Barn Clo	10 B3
Canoe Clo	13 E2
Canterbury Clo	20 B6
Canterbury Rd	15 G4
Captains Walk	25 F4
Carberry Dri	10 B5
Carbis Clo	11 F4

Cardinal Way	
Carisbrook Av	
Carisbrook Rd	
Carless Clo	
Carlton Rd, Gosport	
Carlton Rd, Portchester	
Carlton Way	
Carlyle Rd	
Carnarvon Rd	
Carne Pl	
Caroline Gdns	
Caroline Pl	
Carron Walk	
Cascades App	
Cask St	
Casper John Clo	
Castle Clo	
Castle Gro	
Castle Rd	
Castle St, Portchester	
Castle St, Titchfield	
Castle View Rd	
Catamaran Clo	
Catisfield Rd	
Catsfield La	
Cavanna Clo	
Cawtes Pl	
Cecil Gro	
Cecil Pl	
Cedar Clo	
Cedar Way	
Celandine Av	
Central Rd	
Centre Way	
Chadderton Gdns	
Chaffinch	
Chaffinch Way	
Chale Clo	
Chalk La	
Chalkpit Rd	
Chalky Walk	
Chamberlain Gro	
Chancel Clo	
Chandlers Way	
Chantrell Walk	
Chantry Rd	
Chapel Rd	
Chapel Sq	
Chapel St, Brockhurst	
Chapel St, Portsmouth	
Chapelside	
Charden Rd	
Charfield Clo	
Chark La	
Charlemount Dri	
Charles Dickens St	
Charlesbury Av	
Charlotte Mews	
Charlotte St	
Charnwood	
Chartwell Clo	
Chatfield Rd	
Chatham Dri	
Chatsworth Clo	
Chaucer Av	
Chaucer Clo	
Chedworth Cres	
Cheltenham Cres	
Cheltenham Rd	
Cheriton Rd	
Cherque La	
Cherry Clo	
Cherry Walk	
Cherrygarth Rd	
Cherrytree Av	
Chester Cres	
Chestnut Walk	
Chestnut Way	
Cheviot Walk	
Cheyne Way	
Chichester Clo, Rowner	
Chichester Clo, Warsash	
Chilcombe Clo	
Chilling La	
Chiltern Walk	
Chilworth Gro	
Chine Clo	
Church Clo	
Church La	
Church Path, Fareham	
Church Path, Gosport	
Church Path, Titchfield	
Church Pl	
Church Rd, Alverstoke	
Church Rd, Locks Heath	
Church Rd, Warsash	
Church St	

Name	Ref
ner Clo	22 C2
ner Walk	22 C2
ill Clo	13 G2
ford Clo	11 G2
ar Rd	25 G2
Vay	8 C4
William Rd	19 G5
Clo	13 G2
ce Rd	24 B3
ace St	25 H1
don Cres	13 G2
a Ct	21 F4
all Rd	23 E4
v	7 F5
Clo	11 G3
Ct	5 H6
and Dri	7 G5
and Rd	23 F2
d	18 B1
Rd	19 H6
St	21 F4
r Clo	12 C2
Gro	10 B5
St	25 E3
Clo,	
ks Heath	4 D6
Clo,	
l Common	16 D5
Rd	21 F4
Hill	6 B6
ark La	4 C1
guard Clo	22 D4
en St	21 G5
rell Clo	5 G3
ast Clo	4 D4
ast Way	5 E4
so Rd	8 B4
dge Clo	12 C2
dge Rd	10 D2
bourne Rd	11 F3
on Av	10 C3
e La	25 F3
e Rd	25 E2
e St	25 F3
gton Cres	11 G3
y St	25 G4
oot Dri	4 D6
nead	11 E4
nead Clo	11 F4
nercial Rd	25 H3
non Barn La	19 H5
non Barn Rd	19 H3
non La	6 A6
ton Clo	19 H5
or Av	9 F5
rence Dri	5 F6
er Gro	16 D4
aught La	10 D3
gar Clo	20 C3
ueror Way	19 E1
able Clo	23 G4
be Farm Av	8 B5
be Rd	21 G3
bedale	13 F1
er Gro	10 C5
er St	25 G5
ce Way	7 F3
ns Gro	10 B5
La	20 C1
le Clo	12 D2
Clo	10 B5
Clo	18 C1
orant Clo	9 F5
orant Walk	16 D6
way La	10 A4
eld Rd	8 B2
eld Rd	19 G4
ower Clo	4 D6
vell Clo	20 C3
ada Rd	21 G3
Vay	7 E2
tte Av	13 E2
vold Walk	7 G6
ge Gro, Gosport	23 F1
ge Gro,	
tsmouth	25 H5
s Way	18 C1
sway East	18 C1
ere Rd	21 F4
rry Vw	15 F4
epark Cres	13 H1
Barn Clo	19 G3
Barn La	19 G3
Rd	19 G4
La	10 C5
rd Rd	23 E4
ray Pk	15 E6
s La	12 C5
lip Clo,	
l Common	16 D6
Cowslip Clo, Warsash	12 D1
Coxdale	13 G2
Crableck La	4 B4
Crabthorne Farm La	15 F5
Cranbourne Rd	23 G2
Cranbourne Walk	16 A1
Cranleigh Rd	9 G6
Craven Ct	7 G3
Crawford Dri	7 H2
Credenhill Rd	11 H3
Creek Rd	24 B4
Cremyll Clo	19 E1
Crescent Rd, Fareham	8 B5
Crescent Rd, Gosport	23 E4
Crescent Rd,	
Titchfield Common	13 E1
Crest Clo	9 E4
Crispen Clo	5 F5
Croftlands Av	15 G5
Crofton Av	19 E3
Crofton La	18 C2
Crofton Way	12 A1
Cromerty Clo	15 F5
Cromhall Clo	7 F5
Crompton Way	5 G4
Crooked Walk La	10 D1
Cross Rd	19 H6
Cross St	25 F2
Crossfell Walk	7 G3
Crossland Clo	23 G3
Cuckoo La	15 F5
Culloden Clo	7 H3
Cumber Rd	4 D5
Cumberland St	25 F2
Cunningham Dri,	
Bridgemary	17 F4
Cunningham Dri,	
Locks Heath	5 F5
Curlew Dri	9 F5
Curlew Walk	16 C5
Curtiss Gdns	21 F6
Curzon Howe Rd	25 F3
Cutlers La	15 G5
Cutter Av	12 C1
Cygnet	9 F5
Cyprus Rd	13 G1
Daisy La, Gosport	23 F2
Daisy La, Locks Heath	5 F5
Dale Dri	16 D3
Dale Rd	15 H5
Dalewood Rd	7 F4
Dallington Clo	19 E2
Dampier Clo	20 C3
Dandelion Clo	16 D5
Danes Rd	10 A2
Darren Clo	15 H4
Davis Clo	20 C2
Dayshes Clo	16 D5
Deacon Rd	5 F6
Deal Clo	15 G4
Dean St	25 F3
Deane Gdns	19 H4
Deanes Park Rd	8 D5
Deansgate	19 E1
Deerhurst Cres	11 F2
Defiance Rd	25 F4
Delft Gdns	4 D5
Dell Quay Clo	16 C6
Delme Dri	8 D4
Denbigh Dri	8 A3
Dene Clo	4 D5
Denham Clo	15 G6
Denville Av	10 C5
Derlyn Rd	8 B4
Derwent Clo	15 H4
Derwent Rd	19 G5
Desborough Clo	11 F3
Devonshire Way	7 E6
Dewer Clo	5 G3
Diamond St	25 G5
Diana Clo	22 D2
Dibles Rd	12 C2
Dieppe Gdns	23 E1
Dingle Way	5 F4
Ditton Clo	15 G4
Dock Rd	23 G2
Dolman Rd	23 G3
Dolphin Clo	23 G3
Dolphin Ct	15 F4
Dolphin Way, Clayhall	23 G4
Dolphin Way,	
Portsmouth	25 E4
*Dominie Walk,	
Smeeton Rd	19 G4
Donnelly St	21 F4
Dore Av	10 A3
Dormington Rd	11 G2
Dormy Clo	4 C5
Dormy Way	20 B1
Dorothy Dymond St	25 H3
Dorrien Rd	21 G3
Dorstone Rd	11 H2
Dove Gdns	5 F4
Dover Clo	15 F5
Downend Rd	9 F5
Downland Clo	5 E5
Downside	17 F6
Drake Clo	5 F4
Drake Rd	19 E3
Drift Rd	8 D3
Dryden Av	10 D3
Dugald Drummond St	25 H3
Duisbergy Way	25 G6
Dukes Rd	21 G4
Duncan Dri	6 D6
Duncan Rd	5 F3
Dundee Clo	7 G3
Dunkeld Rd	21 F3
Dunsmore Clo	25 H4
Dunstable Walk	7 F6
Durham St, Brockhurst	21 F4
Durham St, Portsmouth	25 H3
Durley Rd	21 F4
Dursley Cres	11 H4
Eagle Clo	9 F6
Earls Rd	8 B6
Earlsdon St	25 H4
East Cams Clo	9 F5
East Cliff Clo	19 G3
East Hill Clo	8 D4
East House Av	15 H6
East Lodge	7 E5
East St, Fareham	8 C5
East St, Portchester	10 C4
East St, Portsmouth	25 E6
East St, Tichfield	6 C5
East Surrey St	25 H3
Eastbourne Av	21 F2
Eastbrook Clo,	
Brockhurst	21 E2
Eastbrook Clo,	
Locks Heath	5 E3
Eastcroft Rd	21 F5
Eastern Parade	8 C6
Eastern Way	8 C5
Eastfield Av	16 B2
Eden Rise	8 B5
Eden St	25 H2
Edgar Cres	10 C5
Edgecombe Cres	20 B2
Edinburgh Rd	25 G2
Edney Path	4 C3
Edward Gro	10 D2
Eldon St	25 H4
Elgar Clo	23 E4
Elgin Clo	7 H3
Elizabeth Ct	16 B1
Elizabeth Pl	21 H5
Elizabeth Rd	15 H6
Elkstone Rd	11 F2
Ellachie Gdns	23 F4
Ellachie Mews	23 F5
Ellachie Rd	23 F5
Ellerslie Clo	18 C2
Elm Gro, Gosport	23 F1
Elm Gro, Portsmouth	25 H5
Elm St	25 H5
Elmadale Clo	12 C2
Elmhurst Rd, Fareham	8 B5
Elmhurst Rd, Gosport	23 G2
Elmore Av	19 H6
Elmore Clo	19 H5
Elmore Rd	19 H6
Elms Rd	8 B6
Elphinstone Rd	25 H6
Elsfred Rd	18 C1
Elson La	21 F2
Elson Rd	21 F2
Embsay Rd	4 B1
Emmanuel Clo	13 G1
Endeavour Clo	24 B4
Endofield Clo	16 B2
Ennerdale Rd	15 H4
Enterprise Clo	12 C2
Epson Walk	19 H4
Eric Rd	15 G6
Erica Clo	5 E6
Esmonde Clo	19 G4
Esplanade,	
Lee-on-the-Solent	19 F5
Esplanade, Gosport	24 D4
Esplanade,	
Lee-on-the-Solent	19 F5
Ewer Common	23 F3
Exchange Rd	25 G3
Exeter Clo	5 E6
Exmouth Rd	21 F2
Exton Gdns	10 B2
Fairacre Rise	6 D6
Fairacre Walk	6 D6
Fairfield Av	7 G6
Fairholme Clo	21 G3
Fairisle Clo	15 F5
Fairthorne Gdns	21 G6
Fairview Ct	20 D6
Fairwater Clo	20 B1
Falcon Clo	9 F6
Falmouth Rd	11 E3
Fareham Heights	9 E3
Fareham Park Rd	7 E2
Fareham Rd	21 E1
Farm Edge Rd	18 D1
Farm Rd	6 B4
Farmlea	11 E4
Faroes Rd	15 F5
Farrier Way	16 D2
Farriers Walk	23 H1
Farthing La	25 F5
Fastnet Wy	15 F5
Fay Clo	15 G6
Fayre Rd	8 B6
Felix Rd	21 G3
Fell Clo	5 F5
Fell Dri	19 G3
Fern Way	6 A3
Ferncroft Clo	19 E1
Ferndale Mews	16 D4
Ferneham Rd	7 F4
Fernie Clo	15 F6
Ferrol Rd	21 F4
Fey Rd	24 A3
Field Clo, Titchfield	13 F1
Field Clo, Woodcot	16 D3
Fieldmore Rd	21 G3
Filmer Clo	20 C2
Findon Rd	21 G2
Finnisterre Clo	15 F4
Fisguard Rd	21 G3
Fisher Clo	15 G5
Fisher Rd, Bridgemary	17 E5
Fisher Rd, Portsmouth	25 E4
Fishermans Walk	10 C4
Fishers Hill	6 D4
Fitzherbert St	25 H1
Fitzpatrick Ct	11 H3
Fitzwilliam Av	15 E6
Five Post La	21 G4
Flamingo Ct	9 F6
Flathouse Rd	25 H1
Fleet Clo	20 D1
Fleet End Bottom	12 D2
Fleet End Rd	12 D2
Fleming Clo	5 H4
Flint St	25 G5
Font Clo	5 H6
Fontley La	6 C2
Ford Rd	21 F4
Forest Way	20 D1
Forneth Gdns	6 D5
Fort Fareham Rd	16 B2
Fort Rd	23 E4
Forth Clo	15 F5
Forties Clo	15 F4
Forton Rd	23 F1
Foster Clo	15 G4
Foster Rd	23 F2
Founders Way	17 F6
Fountain St	25 H2
Foxbury Gro	10 A5
Foxbury La	17 F4
Foxgloves	8 C2
Foxlea Gdns	21 G3
Foy Gdns	12 B2
Francis Clo	19 H5
Francis Pl	4 B1
Franklin Rd	20 B3
Fraser Rd	17 E4
Frater La	21 F2
Frederick St	25 H1
Freemantle Rd	21 G3
French St	25 F5
Friarspond La	7 E4
Frobisher Clo	20 C4
Frobisher Gro	10 B4
Frogmore	7 E6
Frosthole Clo	7 G2
Frosthole Cres	7 G3
Froxfield Gdns	10 B2
Fulmar Walk	16 C5
Funtley Hill	7 G1
Funtley Rd	7 G1
Furneaux Gdns	8 B2
Fury Way	15 F5
Furzehall Av	8 B2
Gale Moor Av	22 C3
Galleon Clo	12 D1
Garden Courts	10 C4
Garden La	25 H6
Garden Mews	12 B2
Gardner Rd	6 C6
Garland Ct	21 G5
Garnett Clo	15 G4
Garstons Clo	6 B6
Garstons Rd	6 C6
Gatcombe Gdns	7 E5
Gatehouse Rd	10 A5
Gaylyn Way	7 E6
Geoffrey Cres	16 D1
George St	24 A3
Gibralter Clo	7 F4
Gibson Clo	19 H4
Gifford Clo	7 G3
Gilbert Clo	20 D2
Giles Clo, Brockhurst	21 G4
Giles Clo, Fareham	8 B2
Gilkicker Rd	23 G4
Gillcrest	5 G5
Girton Clo	13 G1
Gladstone Gdns	10 B5
Gladstone Rd	21 F3
Glebe Dri	20 C1
Glen Rd	4 D3
Glenbrook Walk	7 F6
Glenda Clo	12 B3
Glendale	13 F1
Glenelg	7 H3
Glenesha Gdns	7 F3
Glenthorne Clo	19 E2
Gloster Ct	5 G4
Gloucester Mews Vw	25 H5
Gloucester Pl	25 H5
Gloucester Rd	25 F2
Gloucester Ter	25 H5
Glyn Dri	15 G6
Glyn Way	15 G6
Godwit Clo	21 H2
Gold St	25 G5
Goldfinch La	19 G3
Gomer La	22 C3
Goodsell Clo	15 F6
Goodwood	13 H1
Goodwood Clo	21 G1
Goodwood Rd	21 G2
Gordon Rd, Brockhurst	21 G6
Gordon Rd, Fareham	8 A4
Gordon Rd, Portsmouth	25 G6
Gorran Av	20 C1
Gorse Clo	12 D1
Gorselands Way	20 C2
Gosport Rd, Fareham	8 B6
Gosport Rd,	
Lee-on-the-Solent	19 H6
Gosport Rd,	
Stubbington	15 H5
Gould Clo	20 D4
Graham Rd	21 F4
Grand Parade	25 F5
Grange Clo	21 F4
Grange Cres	21 F4
Grange La	20 C3
Grange Rd	20 D6
Grasmere Way	15 H4
Grassymead	5 G5
Gray Clo	13 E1
Grays Ct	25 F4
Grayshott Rd	21 F6
Great Gays	18 B1
Great Southsea St	25 G5
Grebe Clo	9 F6
Green Cres	20 C1
Green Crescent La	12 B1
Greenbanks Gdns	8 D4
Greendale Clo	7 F2
Greenhollow Clo	7 H2
Greenlea Gro	21 E3
Greenway Rd	21 G4
Greetham St	25 H3
Gregson Av	17 F5
Gregson Clo	16 D5
Grenadier Clo	5 F6
Grenville Rd	19 F3
Greyfriars Rd	7 E4
Greyshott Av	7 E6
Grindle Clo	10 B2
Grosvenor St	25 H4
Grove Av, Gosport	24 A3
Grove Av, Portchester	10 B6

Grove Blds 23 G2
Grove Rd, Brockhurst 21 G3
Grove Rd, Fareham 8 A4
Grove Rd,
  Lee-on-the-Solent 19 F4
Guardhouse Rd 25 G1
Gudge Heath La 7 F3
Guessens Path 6 C6
Guildhall Sq 25 H3
Guildhall Walk 25 G4
Guillemot Gdns 16 D5
Gull Clo 16 D6
Gullfield Nursery La 5 F2
Gun Wharf Rd 25 F5
Gunners Way 21 F2

Haddon Clo 7 G4
Half Moon St 25 E3
Halfpenny La 25 F5
Hallett Clo 15 G5
Halliday Clo 21 H5
Halsey Clo 23 E2
Ham La 21 G2
Hamble Clo 12 B2
Hamble Rd 21 F6
Hambrook Rd 21 F4
Hambrook St 25 G5
Hamilton Gro 16 D6
Hamilton Rd 10 D4
Hamlet Way 21 F1
Hammond Rd 7 G3
Hampshire Ter 25 G4
Hampton Gro 6 D5
Hanbidge Cres 17 E4
Hanbidge Walk 17 E4
Handley Rd 21 F4
Hanover Ct 25 F5
Hanover Gdns 8 B2
Hanover St 25 F3
Harbour Rd 24 C3
Harbour Tower 24 C4
Harbour Vw 10 B5
Harcourt Rd, Gosport 21 G5
Harcourt Rd, Titchfield 6 D6
Harding Rd 21 F4
Hardy Clo 5 F4
Harebell Clo 8 C2
Harlequin Gro 7 H4
Harold Rd 15 H5
Harrier Clo 19 H4
Harriet Clo 15 F6
Harris Rd 17 E4
Harrison Rd 8 B3
Harting Gdns 10 B2
Hartington Rd 21 F4
Hartlands Rd 8 B5
Harvester Dri 6 D4
Harvey Cres 13 E1
Harwood Clo 17 E4
Harwood Rd 17 E4
Haselworth Dri 23 F5
Haslar Bri 24 C5
Haslar Rd 24 B6
Haslar Sea Wall 23 H4
Hastings Av 21 F2
Hatherley Cres 9 H6
Hatherley Dri 9 H6
Hatherley Rd 11 F3
Havant St 25 E3
Havelock Rd 12 B2
Haven Cres 18 B1
Hawk Clo 15 F6
Hawke St 25 F3
Hawkins Rd 17 F6
Hawkwell 9 F5
Hawthorn Gdns 10 B3
Hawthorn La 4 C3
Hawthorn Walk 19 G4
Hay St 25 G3
Hayes Clo 7 F2
Hayling Clo 7 F6
Hazel Gro 5 G6
Hazelwood 15 F3
Headland Dri 5 E5
Heath La 14 C1
Heath Lawns 7 F5
Heath Rd 5 E6
Heath Rd North 4 D5
Heath Rd South 4 D6
Heather Clo 16 D6
Heather Gdns 7 F3
Heathfield Av 7 F5
Heaton Rd 21 F3
Hebrides Clo 15 F5
Hedley Clo 19 H4
Hedra Clo 5 E6
Helsby Clo 7 G6
Helsted Clo 22 C2
Helston Rd 11 E3
Hempstead Rd 11 G3

Henley Gdns 7 G2
Henry St 24 B4
Henville Clo 20 D2
Herbert Rd 21 F5
Heron Way 16 D5
Herons Clo 15 G4
Hertsfield 5 G5
Heston Walk 22 C2
Hewett Clo 6 C6
Hewett Rd 6 C6
Hewitts Rise 12 B3
Hewitt Clo 21 F4
Hickley Path 8 D3
High Dri 20 B1
High Mead 7 G2
High Oaks Clo 5 E6
High St, Bursledon 4 A2
High St, Fareham 8 C4
High St, Gosport 24 C4
High St,
  Lee-on-the-Solent 19 G5
High St, Portsmouth 25 F5
High St, Titchfield 6 C5
High Vw 10 B2
High Walk 7 G2
Highbury St 25 F5
Highcliff Rd 21 F6
Highfield Av 7 H6
Highfield Rd 21 F4
Highfields 12 D1
Highlands Rd 7 E5
Highnam Gdns 5 E5
Highwood Rd 20 C3
Hill Coppice Rd 5 H4
Hill Dri 7 G3
Hill Head Rd 18 B1
Hill Park Rd, Brockhurst 21 E4
Hill Park Rd, Hill Park 7 F2
Hill Pl 4 A1
Hill Rd 10 B2
Hill View Rd 10 B3
Hill Walk 7 F3
Hillary Clo 7 H3
Hillbrow Clo 7 G2
Hillcroft 6 A2
Hiller Walk 19 H4
Hillside Cres 10 D3
Hillsley Rd 11 E2
Hillson Dri 7 E2
Hilton Rd 23 G3
Hobbs Passage 24 C4
Hoeford Clo 16 D2
Holbrook Rd 8 B5
Hollam Clo 6 D5
Hollam Cres 6 D5
Hollam Dri 6 D5
Holland Pk 4 D5
Holland Pl 17 E6
Holly Clo 4 C5
Holly Gro 7 G2
Holly Hill La 4 B5
Holly St 24 A4
Hollybank 19 G5
Hollybrook Gdns 5 F4
Holmdale Rd 21 F3
Holmefield Av 16 B2
Holmgrove 5 G6
Home Rule Rd 5 F5
Homer Clo 20 B2
Honey La 7 F1
Honeysuckle Clo,
  Park Gate 5 F4
Honeysuckle Clo,
  Peel Common 16 D5
Hood Clo 5 F5
Hook La 13 E3
Hook Park Rd 12 B4
Hope St 25 H2
Hornby Clo 12 C3
Hornet Clo, Fareham 7 F3
Hornet Clo, Gosport 23 G3
Horseshoe Clo 6 A4
Horseshoe Lodge 12 D1
Horton Rd 17 E4
Hospital La 10 D6
House Farm Rd 21 E6
Howe Rd 20 C5
Howerts Clo 12 C3
Hoylake Clo 20 C1
Hoylecroft Clo 7 G2
Humber Clo 15 F5
Hunter Clo 20 D3
Hunters Lodge 7 E5
Huntingdon Clo 13 G2
Huntley Clo 11 G3
Hunts Pond Rd 13 G1
Hurst Clo 18 C1
Hurst Grn 16 D6
Huxley Clo 13 G1
Hyde St 25 H5

Ilex Cres 5 E6
INDUSTRIAL ESTATES:
  Apple Ind Est 5 G4
  Barratt Ind Est 5 G4
  Brockhurst Ind Site 21 F1
  Castle Trading Est 10 D4
  Fareham Ind Park 8 D3
  Fort Fareham Ind Site 16 C2
  Newgate Lane Ind Est 16 C2
  Segensworth East
    Ind Est 5 H4
  Segensworth West
    Ind Est 5 G4
  Solent 2 Bus. Park 5 G2
  Speedfields Park 16 C3
Ingledene Clo 23 F2
Ingleside Clo 6 D6
Inverkip Clo 19 F3
Inverness Av 7 G3
Inverness Rd 21 G4
Iron Mill Clo 7 F2
Iron Mill La 6 D1
Irvine Clo 8 A2
Isambard Brunel Rd 25 H3
Island View Walk 10 B2
Ivy La 25 F1

Jacobs St 25 H2
Jacomb Pl 17 F6
Jago Rd 25 E2
Jamaica Rd 23 G2
James Clo 17 E4
James Grieve Av 5 F6
James Rd 16 D4
Java Dri 5 G2
Jarvis Fields 4 A1
Jasmine Walk 7 G5
Jason Way 21 E2
Jellicoe Av 22 D4
Jerram Clo 22 D3
Jersey Clo 19 E2
Jervis Dri 21 G4
Jesmond Gro 13 F1
Jessie Rd 21 F6
Johns Rd 8 B6
Jonathan Rd 7 G4
Joseph St 24 A4
Jubilee Av 10 D3
Jubilee Ct 16 C1
Jubilee Rd, Gosport 21 G5
Jubilee Rd, Portchester 10 C4
Jubilee Ter 25 G5
Julie Av 7 G4
Jumar Clo 12 B3
Justin Clo 7 G5
Jute Clo 10 B3

Kealy Rd 21 G4
Keast Walk 17 E4
Keats Av 10 D2
Keilder Gro 17 F6
Keith Clo 21 G4
Kelsey Clo 13 F1
Kelsey Head 11 F4
Kelvin Gro 10 C3
Kenilworth Clo 19 G4
Kennedy Av 7 G2
Kennedy Cres 22 D4
Kennet Clo 23 F4
Kensington Rd 23 G2
Kent Gro 10 B5
Kent Rd, Portsmouth 25 G4
Kent Rd, Woodcot 16 D4
Kent St 25 F3
Kenwood Rd 10 C6
Kenya Rd 10 A4
Kestrel Clo 15 G4
Keyes Clo 17 E4
Keyes Rd 17 E5
Keyhaven Clo 16 C6
Kilmiston Dri 10 B2
Kiln Acre 8 B3
Kiln Rd 7 H2
Kilwich Way 10 A5
Kimpton Clo 19 H4
King Charles St 25 F3
King George Rd 10 B4
King Henry I St 25 G3
King John Av 10 A4
King Richard I Rd 25 G3
King St, Gosport 24 B3
King St, Portsmouth 25 F2
King William St 25 F1
Kingcup Av 5 H4
Kingdom Clo 5 H4
Kingfisher Copse 5 F4
Kingfishers 9 F6
Kings Rd, Fareham 8 B5
Kings Rd, Gosport 23 F1

Kings Rd,
  Lee-on-the-Solent 19 F4
Kings Rd, Portsea 25 E2
Kings Rd, Portsmouth 25 G5
Kings Ter 25 G5
Kingsbench Alley 25 F3
Kingscote Rd 11 E2
Kingsland Clo 11 H3
Kingsley Rd 21 F3
Kingsmead Av 19 E2
Kingsmill Clo 23 E2
Kingston Gdns 7 F1
Kingston Rd 21 F5
*Kingswell Path,
  Commercial Rd 25 H3
Kingswell St 25 H2
Kitescroft Clo 13 H2
Kittewake Clo 16 D6
Kneller Ct 7 H2
Knights Bank Rd 18 B1
Knotgrass Rd 12 D1
Kyak Clo 12 D2
Kynon Clo 21 H2

Laburnum Rd 16 D1
Ladram Rd 22 D2
Lakeside, Fareham 7 G1
Lakeside,
  Lee-on-the-Solent 19 G6
Lambourn Clo 7 F5
Lambourne Dri 5 F6
Lancaster Clo,
  Lee-on-the-Solent 20 A6
Lancaster Clo,
  Portchester 10 A2
Landon Rd 20 D2
Landport St 25 G4
Landport Ter 25 G4
Landport Vw 25 H2
Lands End Rd 4 A1
Lanes End 15 G6
Langstone Walk,
  Fareham 7 F6
Langstone Walk,
  Rowner 16 D6
Lansdown Av 10 C6
Lansdowne St 25 G4
Lapthorn Clo 16 D4
Lapwing Clo 21 H3
Lapwing Gro 9 F4
Larch Clo 19 H5
Larchdale Clo 12 C3
Larches Gdns 7 E5
Larkspur Clo 12 D1
Laser Clo 12 D1
Lasham Walk 7 F6
Laurel Clo 5 F5
Laurel Gdns 5 F5
Laurel Rd 5 F5
Laurus Walk 19 H4
Laverock La 10 B3
Lavinia Rd 23 F1
Lawn Clo 20 D2
Lawn Dri 13 F1
Lawrence Rd 7 H4
Lawson Clo 4 C1
Laxton Clo 5 F6
Layton Rd 17 E5
Leabrook 24 D4
Leamington Cres 19 G4
Lear Rd 23 F1
Lechlade Gdns 7 G1
Leckford Clo 10 B2
Ledbury Rd 11 G3
Lederle La 17 E3
Lee Rd 21 G4
Leep La 23 F4
Lees La 21 G5
Leesland Rd 21 F5
Leigh Rd 8 A4
Leith Av 10 C3
Lennox Clo 23 G5
Lennox Row 25 F2
Leominster Rd 11 F2
Leonard Rd 23 G1
Leopard St 25 F3
Lerryn Rd 17 F6
Lester Rd 21 E5
Leventhorpe Ct 23 G2
Leviathan Clo 15 H6
Levison Clo 22 D3
Leyland Clo 23 F3
Lichfield Rd 5 G6
Lime Gro 11 F2
Lincoln Clo 5 G6
Lind Clo 23 G5
Lind Way 5 E3
Linden Gro 23 F2
Linden Lea 10 B3
Link Way 19 E2

Linnet Ct
Lion St
Lion Ter
Little Abshot Rd
Little Anglesey Rd
Little Britain St
Little Chilworth
Little Clo
Little Gays
Little Green
Little Green Orchard
Little La
Little Park Farm Rd
Little Southsea St
Littlewood Gdns
Lock App
Lock View
Locks Heath Park Rd
Locks Rd
Lockswood Rd
Lodge Gdns
Lodge Rd
Lombard St
Lombardy Clo
Long Curtain Rd
Long Drive
Longacres
Longdean Clo
Longfield Av
Longmynd Dri
Longs La
Longstaffe Gdns
Longwater Dri
Lonsdale Av
Lord Montgomery Way
Lovett Gro
Lower Bellfield
Lower Church Path
Lower Church Rd
Lower Duncan Rd
Lower Quay
Lower Quay Rd
Lower Spinney
Lower Swanwick Rd
Ludlow Rd
Lulworth Rd
Lundy Walk
Lychgate Grn
Lydney Clo
Lydney Rd
Lyndale Rd
Lynden Clo
Lyndhurst Rd
Lynton Gdns

Mabey Clo
Macaulay Av
Madden Clo
Maddison Ct
Madison Clo
Magdalene Way
Magennis Clo
Magnolia Clo
Magpie La
Main Rd
Main Rd
Maizemore Walk
Malcolm Clo
Malin Clo
Mallard Gdns
Mallory Cres
Mallow Clo
Malt House La
Malvern Av
Malvern Rd
Mancroft Av
Manor Ct
Manor Way
Mansfield Rd
Mantle Clo
Maple Clo, Fareham
Maple Clo,
  Lee-on-the-Solent
Margarita Rd
Margerys Ct
Marigold Clo
Marina Keep
Marina Gro
Marine Parade East
Marine Parade West
Mariners Way, Gosport
Mariners Way,
  Warsash
Market Way
Marks Rd
Marks Tey Rd
Marlborough Gro
Marlborough Rd
Marlborough Row

...es Clo	20 D2
...ow Clo	7 G1
...den Rd	11 G3
...h La	15 E6
...ello Clo	22 C3
...ells Ct	25 F4
...ha St	25 H1
...n Av	15 H6
...n Clo	19 G3
...Rose Clo	7 G2
...field Av	10 D2
...en Cres	20 C2
...ield Clo	15 H5
...ield Rd	23 G3
...lower Clo	19 E1
...ings Farm Rd	7 H3
...hard Clo	17 E4
...idge	5 G5
...s La	15 G5
...ree Clo	5 E6
...ree Gdns	8 A5
...ree Rd	8 A5
...d Way	8 B3
...dcroft Clo	12 B3
...dow Av	5 F5
...dow St	25 G5
...dow Walk	16 D3
...dowbank Rd	7 F4
...ourne St	25 H4
...ose Gdns	21 E3
...ille Rd	21 G3
...dips Rd	7 G6
...dips Walk	7 F6
...n Clo	16 D6
...n Rd	14 C4
...ganser Clo	21 H3
...den Rd	25 G4
...sn Gdns	10 B2
...ow Clo	9 G5
...yfield	5 G5
...stone Rd	17 E6
...on Av	10 C6
...on Cres	10 C5
...le Mead	6 D6
...le Rd	5 F4
...le St	25 H4
...lecroft La	21 F4
...leton Clo	7 G6
...leton Walk	7 G6
...eld Clo	16 B1
...ways	18 D1
...End Rd	25 F4
...ary Rd, Downend	9 E3
...ary Rd, Portsmouth	25 G1
...ary Rd, Privett	20 D6
...ary Rd, Wallington	8 D3
...La, Forton	21 H4
...La, Portsmouth	25 H1
...La, Titchfield	6 C3
...Pond Rd	21 G4
...Rd, Brockhurst	21 F4
...Rd, Fareham	8 B6
...St	6 C5
...r Dri	7 H2
...n Gro	13 G1
...ll Rd	19 F4
...or Clo	13 E1
...hell Clo	5 H4
...Dri	22 C2
...Walk	22 C2
...sworth Rd	23 G2
...arch Clo	13 F1
...ckton Rd	23 F5
...ks Hill	19 E3
...ks Way	18 C2
...roe Clo	22 C2
...tgomery Rd	17 E4
...trose Av	10 D2
...tserrat Rd	19 F4
...ument La	9 H1
...dy Rd	18 D1
...re Gdns	21 F6
...aunt Clo	21 H2
...aunt Dri	10 A5
...eland Rd	5 E5
...eland Rd	23 F1
...gans Dri	15 G3
...ningside Av	10 D3
...is Clo	16 D3
...shead Cres	8 A3
...imer Rd	11 G3
...more Rd	21 F4
...nd Clo	23 E2
...nt Clo	6 D5
...nt Pleasant Rd	23 F3
...ntbatten Clo	17 E4
...ntview Av	10 D3
...sehole Rd	11 E3
...erry Av	19 E2
...erry Clo	23 F2
Mumby Rd	24 B3
Murray Clo	7 G3
Murrays La	25 E2
Museum Rd	25 G5
Myrtle Av	10 C4
Myrtle Clo	16 D5
Nailsworth Rd	11 G3
Naish Dri	21 G1
Napier Cres	7 E4
Naseby Clo	11 F2
Nashe Clo	7 F3
Nashe Way	7 E3
Nasmith Clo	22 C2
Navy Rd	25 F1
Neelands Gro	10 D4
Nelson Av	10 A4
Nelson Ct	16 B2
Nelson La	10 B1
Nelson Rd	23 F2
Nepean Clo	8 A5
Neptune Rd	7 F3
Nesbitt Clo	16 D5
Netherton Rd	21 F3
Netley Rd	13 G1
Neville Av	10 C5
Neville Ct	23 F1
New Rd, Fareham	8 B4
New Rd, Sarisbury	25 H4
New Rd, Warsash	12 C3
Newbolt Rd	20 D2
Newbroke Rd	20 D2
Newgate La	16 C5
Newgate Rd	16 C5
Newlands Av	21 F6
Newlyn Way	11 F4
Newport Rd	21 E5
Newton Clo	15 G3
Newton Pl	19 F4
Newtown	10 C3
Newtown Rd	12 B3
Nicholas Cres	7 H4
Nicholl Pl	17 E6
Nickel St	25 G5
Nightingale Clo	21 E4
Nightingale Rd	25 G6
Nimrod Dri	20 C4
Nine Elms La	8 D1
Niton Clo	17 E6
Nobbs La	25 F4
Nobes Av	17 E5
Nobes Clo	17 F6
Norfolk Rd	21 E3
Norfolk St	25 H5
Norgett Way	10 B5
Norman Clo	10 C5
Norman Rd	21 F5
Normandy Clo	23 E1
Norset Rd	7 F3
North Clo	22 D2
North Cross St	24 C4
North Hill	8 B2
North Path	20 C4
North St, Gosport	7 H2
North St, Portsmouth	25 F2
North Wallington	8 C3
Northarbour Rd	11 H4
Northarbour Spur	11 H4
Northcott Clo	23 E3
Northcroft Rd	21 F4
Northfield Av	16 B1
Northfield Park	9 H4
Northmore Clo	5 F4
Northmore Rd	5 F4
Northway, Bridgemary	17 E4
Northways, Stubbington	15 H6
Northwood Sq	8 B4
Norton Dri	8 A3
Norwich Clo	4 C5
Norwich Pl	19 F3
Nottingham Pl	19 F4
Nursery Clo	16 D5
Nursery La	19 E1
Nutash	5 G5
Nyewood Clo	10 C2
Nyria Way	23 H2
Oak Rd	7 F4
Oak St	24 A4
Oakcroft La	15 G3
Oakdene	20 D1
Oakdown Rd	15 H5
Oaklands Gdns	13 G2
Oaklands Way	13 G2
Oakwood Clo	12 C3
Occupation La	6 A6
Ocean Clo	7 F3
Ockenden Clo	25 H5
Odell Clo	7 H2
Olave Clo	19 G4
Old Commercial Rd	25 H1
Old Common	5 F5
Old Common Gdns	5 E5
Old Farm La	18 D1
Old Garden Clo	5 G6
Old Gosport Rd	8 B6
Old Rd	23 G3
Old St	15 E6
Old Swanwick La	4 B1
Old Turnpike	8 B2
Oldbury Way	7 F5
Oldstar Pl	25 E3
Oleander Clo	5 F4
Olive Cres	10 C5
Orange Gro	20 D1
Orchard Clo	21 F1
Orchard Gro	10 A5
Orchard Rd	13 E1
Ordnance Rd	24 B4
Ordnance Row	25 F3
Oriel Dri	13 G2
Orion Clo	15 H6
Orwell Cres	13 G1
Osborn Cres	16 D4
Osborn Rd	8 B4
Osborn Rd South	8 B4
Osborne Rd, Lee-on-the-Solent	19 F4
Osborne Rd, Newtown	12 B3
Osborne View Rd	18 C1
Oslands La	4 B2
Osprey Clo	19 H4
Osprey Ct	9 F5
Oval Gdns	22 D2
Owen Clo	20 C3
Oxford Clo	8 A3
Oxford Rd	21 E5
Oxleys Clo	6 D6
Oyster Mews	25 F5
Oyster Quay	11 F5
Oyster St	25 F5
Paddock Walk	11 E4
Paffard Clo	20 C3
Paget Rd	25 G6
Painswick Clo, Paulsgrove	11 G3
Painswick Clo, Sarisbury	4 D3
Pallant Gdns	8 D4
Palmerston Av	8 C4
Palmerston Dri	16 C1
Palmerston Rd	25 H6
Palmerston Way	22 D4
Palmyra Rd	21 G3
Pamela Av	11 E3
Pan St	25 H2
Pannall Rd	21 F3
Paradise La	9 E4
Paradise St	25 H2
Parham Rd	21 H4
Park Clo	21 E4
Park Farm Av	7 F2
Park La, Fareham	8 B4
Park La, Stubbington	15 G5
Park Rd, Alverstoke	23 F3
Park Rd, Portsmouth	25 F4
Park St, Gosport	23 F1
Park St, Portsmouth	25 G4
Park Walk	7 F3
Parker Clo	21 F1
Parkglen	5 G5
Parklands	5 E5
Parklands Clo	21 G4
Parklands Ct	21 E6
Parr Rd	11 H4
Passage La	12 A2
Patchway Dri	7 F5
Paxton Rd	8 A5
Peacock La	25 F5
Peak Dri	7 F5
Peak La	7 F6
Peartree Clo	15 H5
Peel Rd	24 A3
Pelham Rd, Gosport	21 G5
Pelham Rd, Portsmouth	25 H5
Pelican Clo	7 F3
Pembroke Clo, Lee-on-the-Solent	19 G6
Pembroke Cres	18 C1
Pembroke Clo	5 F4
Pembury Rd	15 H3
Pendennis Rd	21 F2
Penhale Gdns	13 F2
Penn Way	20 A4
Pennine Walk	7 G6
Pennine Way	20 A6
Pennington Way	7 F2
Penny St	25 F5
Pennycress	12 D1
Pentland Rise	10 C2
Pepys Clo	23 F5
Percy Rd	23 G2
Pershore Clo	5 F6
Perth Rd	17 E5
Peters Clo	4 D6
Peters Rd	4 D6
Petrel Walk	16 D6
Petrie Rd	19 G4
Pettycot Cres	16 D5
Pier Rd	25 G6
Pier St	19 F5
Pilgrims Way	18 D2
Pilning Clo	7 F5
Pimpernel Clo	4 D6
Pine Walk	5 E3
Pinetrees Clo	7 F5
Pinewood, Brockhurst	21 E1
Pinewood, Rowner	20 D1
Pinewood Clo	15 H4
Pinks Hill	8 D4
Pipit Clo	21 H3
Pitchponds Rd	12 B3
Place House Clo	7 E4
Plover Clo	15 F5
Plymouth Dri	15 E6
Pond Rd	4 D3
Pook La	8 B1
Poplar Dri	7 G6
Port Solent	11 E5
Port Way	11 G5
Portal Rd	17 E5
Portchester La	10 C1
Portchester Rd	8 D5
Portland Dri	22 C3
Portland Rd	25 H6
Portland St, Fareham	8 C5
Portland St, Portsmouth	25 F3
Portobello Gro	10 C3
Portsdown Hill Rd	10 A1
Portsdown Rd	10 D4
Portsmouth Rd	20 A6
Portsview Av	10 C3
Portsview Gdns	10 C3
Posbrook La	14 C3
Postern Clo	10 C4
Potters Av	8 A2
Pound Clo	20 D2
Poundgate Dri	13 G2
Poynings Pl	25 F5
Prelate Way	13 H1
Prideaux-Brune Av	17 E4
Primate Rd	13 H1
Primrose Clo	17 E3
Primrose Way	12 D1
Prince Alfred St	23 F2
Prince George St	25 F2
Prince of Wales Rd	24 B4
Prinsted Walk	11 F4
Priory Rd, Elson	21 G2
Priory Rd, Fareham	7 F4
Privett Pl	21 E6
Privett Rd, Hill Park	7 E3
Privett Rd, Privett	22 A2
Puffin Cres	15 F4
Puffin Gdns	16 D5
Pump La	20 C1
Purbeck Dri	7 F6
Purbeck St	25 F3
Purbeck Walk	7 F6
Pye St	25 H2
Pyrford Clo	22 C2
Pytchley Clo	15 E6
Quay Haven	4 B1
Quay La	21 G1
Quay St	8 C5
Queen Mary Rd	10 C4
Queen St	25 E3
Queens Clo	19 F4
Queens Cres, Southsea	25 H6
Queens Cres, Stubbington	15 H5
Queens Gro	25 H6
Queens Pl	25 H6
Queens Rd, Fareham	8 B5
Queens Rd, Gosport	23 G1
Queens Rd, Lee-on-the-Solent	19 G6
Queens Rd, Portsea	25 E2
Queens Rd, Warsash	12 B2
Queens Way	25 H6
Quintrell Av	9 G6
Racecourse La	11 G4
Radclyffe Rd	8 D3
Radnor St	25 H4
Raley Rd	13 E1
Rampart Row	24 C5
Ramsay Pl	17 E6
Rannoch Clo	7 G3
Ransome Clo	6 B6
Ranvilles La	6 D6
Rapson Clo	11 H3
Ravens Clo	15 H5
Ravenswood	5 G6
Raymond Rd	10 D3
Raynes Rd	19 H6
Rectory Clo, Alverstoke	23 E4
Rectory Clo, Stubbington	15 G5
Red Barn La	7 G1
Redbarn Av	10 B3
Redlands La	8 A5
Redwood Dri	10 A3
Reeds Pl	21 G4
Reeds Rd	21 G3
Regent Pl	25 G6
Repton Clo	22 C2
Richard Gro	21 F1
Richards Clo	5 F5
Richmond Pl	25 F3
Richmond Rd, Lee-on-the-Solent	19 F4
Richmond Rd, Privett	21 G6
Richmond Rise	10 B3
Ridgeway Clo	11 E2
Riverside Av	8 D3
Roberts Rd	21 E4
Robins Clo	15 G5
Robins Meadow	13 G2
Robinson Ct	10 B3
Robinson Rd	18 D1
Rockingham Way	9 H5
Rodney Clo	20 C4
Rogate Gdns	10 B2
Rogers Rd	21 G4
Roman Gro	10 C6
Romford Rd	12 B3
Romsey Av	9 G5
Rookery Av	5 G2
Rooksway Gro	9 F5
Rosedale Clo	6 B5
Rosemary La	25 F3
Rosemary Walk	19 G4
Rosewood	20 D1
Ross Way	19 G4
Rossan Av	12 B3
Rothesay Rd	21 F3
Rothwell Clo	11 F3
Row Wood La	20 B1
Rowallen Av	20 B2
Rowan Clo	19 H5
Rowan Way	7 E6
Rowe Ash Way	5 E5
Rowland Rd, Fareham	7 H4
Rowland Rd, Portchester	10 D3
Rowner Clo	20 C1
Rowner La	20 C2
Rowner Rd	20 A1
Rudgwick Clo	9 G5
Runnymead	7 F2
Russell Clo	19 G4
Russell Pl	8 B4
Russell Rd	19 G5
Russell St	21 G4
Rydal Rd	21 F2
Ryde Pl	19 H6
Ryecroft	5 G6
Sackville St	25 H4
St Andrews Rd	23 F2
St Annes Gro	7 H6
St Anns Cres	21 F4
St Catherines Way	9 E5
St Christopher Av	8 C3
St Christopher Gdns	17 E6
St Cuthberts Clo	5 F5
St Cuthberts La	5 F5
St Davids Rd	4 D6
St Edmunds Clo	13 G2
St Edwards Rd, Gosport	23 F2
St Edwards Rd, Southsea	25 H5
St Faiths Clo	23 E1
St Francis Rd	23 G5
St Georges Rd, Portsmouth	25 F4
St Georges Rd, Sarisbury	4 D6
St Georges Sq	25 F3
St Georges Way	25 F3
St Helena Way	10 B4
St Helens Rd	22 C3
St James's Rd	25 H4
St James's St	25 F3
St Johns Clo	23 F1
St Johns Rd	5 F6
St Johns Sq	21 G5
St Joseph Clo	5 F5

St Judes Clo 25 H6
St Leonards Clo 6 B2
St Lukes Rd 21 F4
St Margarets La 6 B4
St Marks Clo 23 F4
St Marks Pl 23 F4
St Marks Rd 23 F4
St Marys Av 23 E3
St Marys Rd 15 G4
St Michaels Gro 7 H6
St Michaels Rd,
  Locks Heath 5 E6
St Michaels Rd,
  Portsmouth 25 G4
St Nicholas Av 20 B2
St Nicholas St 25 F5
St Pauls Rd,
  Portsmouth 25 G4
St Pauls Rd, Sarisbury 4 D3
St Pauls Sq 25 G4
St Sebastian Cres 8 C3
St Simon Clo 5 F5
St Thomas a Becket Ct 25 F5
St Thomas Clo 8 C3
St Thomas's Ct 25 F5
St Thomas's Rd 21 G2
St Thomas's St 25 F5
St Tristan Clo 5 F6
St Valerie Rd 23 F3
St Vincent Rd 21 G4
Salerno Clo 21 F6
Salisbury Ter 19 G5
Salterns 8 C6
Salterns La 16 D1
Salterns Rd 18 C2
Sampson Rd 25 E2
Samson Clo 20 C3
San Diego Rd 21 G4
Sandcroft Clo 22 C3
Sandford Av 22 C2
Sandhill La 20 A3
Sandisplatt 7 E6
Sandown Clo 22 C3
Sandport Gro 10 A5
Sandringham Rd 7 E5
Sandy La 6 B6
Sandycroft 12 B2
Sanross Clo 18 C1
Savage Clo 20 D4
Savernake Clo 17 F6
Saville Clo 22 D2
Saville Gdns 8 A2
Saxon Clo, Fleet End 12 C1
Saxon Clo, Portchester 10 B2
Scafell Av 7 F6
School Rd 21 C1
Schooner Way 12 C2
Scott Clo 15 G4
Scott Rd, Portsea 25 E2
Scott Rd, Southsea 25 F4
Sea Crest Rd 19 G5
Sea Horse Ct 24 C3
Sea Horse Walk 23 H1
Sea Kings 15 F5
Sea La 19 E2
Sea Mill Gdns 25 F3
Sea Mill Path 25 F3
Seabird Way 8 B6
Seafield Park Rd 18 C2
Seafield Rd 10 A5
Seagers Ct 25 E5
Seamead 19 E2
Seaton Clo 19 E1
Seaview Av 10 D3
Seaward Tower 24 C5
Seaway Gro 10 B5
Sedgefield Clo 10 D4
Sedgeley Gro 21 F2
Sedgewick Clo 20 B2
Segensworth Rd 6 A2
Selborne Gdns 21 F6
Selsey Av 21 F2
Sennen Pl 11 F5
Sephton Clo 20 C4
Serpentine Rd 8 B3
Severn Clo, Downend 9 G5
Severn Clo, Paulsgrove 11 G2
Seymour Rd 19 H6
Shackleton Rd 20 C3
Shaftesbury Rd,
  Gosport 23 G2
Shaftesbury Rd,
  Southsea 25 H6
Shalbourne Rd 21 F3
Shamrock Clo 24 B4
Shannon Clo 7 F4
Shannon Rd 15 F5
Sharpness Clo 7 F6
Shearwater Clo 16 D6
Shellcroft 12 B2

Shelley Av 10 D3
Shenley Clo 7 E4
Shepards Clo 7 E6
Shepherds Purse Clo 4 D6
Sherwin Walk 23 E3
Sherwood Gdns 4 C5
Sherwood Rd 21 F6
Shoot La 20 A2
Shore Rd 12 A2
Short Rd 18 C1
Short Row 25 F2
Sibland Clo 7 F5
Silver Birch Av 7 G5
Silver St 25 G5
Simpson Clo 10 B3
Sissinghurst Rd 10 A5
Skew Rd 10 B2
Skipper Way 19 G5
Skylark Way 19 G3
Slindon St 25 H3
Slingsby Clo 25 G5
Sloetree Clo 13 G1
Smeeton Rd 19 G4
Smith St 21 G5
Snap Dragon Clo 12 D1
Snape Clo 20 B2
Snowdon Dri 7 G6
Solent Dri 12 C4
Solent Rd 18 C1
Solent Vw 10 B3
Solent Way 22 D3
Somervell Clo 23 E4
Somervell Dri 8 A3
Sorrel Clo 12 D1
South Clo 22 D3
South Cross St 24 C4
South Lodge 7 E5
South Normandy 25 F4
South Path 20 C5
South Pl 19 H6
South St, Gosport 24 A5
South St, Portsmouth 25 G5
South St, Titchfield 6 C5
South Ter 25 E2
Southampton Hill 6 C5
Southampton Rd,
  Fareham 8 B4
Southampton Rd,
  Park Gate 5 G4
Southampton Rd,
  Portchester 10 D4
Southampton Row 25 F3
Southcliff Clo 19 G4
Southcroft Rd 21 E5
Southmead Rd 7 F4
Southsea Ter 25 G6
Southway, Bridgemary 17 E4
Southway, Titchfield 6 B3
Southways 15 H6
Southwick Av 10 D2
Southwick Ct 16 C1
Southwick Rd 11 G1
Southwood Gdns 4 D6
Sparrow Ct 19 H3
Speedwell Clo 12 D1
Spencer Ct 16 A6
Spencer Dri 19 H5
Spenser Clo 12 C3
Spithead Av 23 G5
Spring Ct 19 G5
Spring Garden La 24 B4
Spring Gdns 25 G3
Spring Rd 4 D3
Spring St 25 H2
Springcroft 16 D3
Springfield Way 19 E2
Spruce Clo 12 C2
Spruce Walk 19 G4
Spurlings Rd 8 D1
Stable Clo 6 A4
Standard Way 8 C2
Stanford Clo 11 H3
Stanhope Rd 25 H3
Stanley Clo, Elson 21 G1
Stanley Clo, Fareham 7 G4
Staplers Reach 20 B1
Stares Clo 20 C3
Station App 19 E2
Station Hill 4 A1
Station Rd, Brockhurst 21 E3
Station Rd, Bursledon 4 A1
Station Rd, Portchester 10 C3
Station Rd, Swanwick 5 F3
Station St 25 H3
Steel St 25 G5
Steep Clo 10 B2
Steeple Way 5 H6
Stephen Rd 7 H4
Stephenson Clo 23 E4
Stirling Ct 7 G3

Stocker Pl 20 D1
Stoke Gdns 23 G2
Stoke Rd 23 F2
Stokes Bay Rd 22 C4
Stone La 23 F2
Stone St 25 G5
Stoneleigh Clo 9 H6
Stoner Clo 16 D5
Stony La 25 E2
Stowe Estate 7 F3
Stradbrook 20 B1
Strathmore Rd 24 A4
Stratton Clo 11 H3
Strawberry Hill 4 D5
Streamleaze 13 G1
Stroud Green La 15 H3
Stuart Clo 19 E1
Stubbington Grn 15 G5
Stubbington La 19 E1
Studland Rd 19 G5
Suffolk Dri 5 G1
Sumar Clo 15 H3
Summerfields 13 F1
Sun St 25 F3
Sunbeam Way 23 F3
Sunbury Ct 7 G2
Sunningdale Clo 20 C1
Sunningdale Rd 10 C4
Sunny Walk 25 E2
Surrey St 25 H3
Sussex Pl 25 H6
Sussex Rd 25 H6
Sussex Ter 25 H6
Swallow Ct 19 G3
Swallow Wood 8 B2
Swanage Rd 19 F4
Swancote 9 F5
Swanwick La 4 B1
Swanwick Shore Rd 4 B2
Swift Clo 19 G3
Swivelton La 9 G1
Sword Clo 22 D3
Sycamore Clo, Rowner 20 D1
Sycamore Clo,
  Titchfield Common 13 G2
Sydney Rd 23 F1
Tait Pl 20 D1
Tallan Rd 13 F2
Tamar Clo 9 G5
Tamarisk Clo 19 E2
Tammys Turn 6 D6
Tamworth Pl 23 G2
Tanglewood 8 A2
Tanner La 16 A2
Tanyges Clo 15 H5
Tarius Clo 17 F5
Tarleton Rd 11 G3
Tatershall Cres 10 A5
Teal Clo 9 F6
Teal Walk 16 D5
Tedder Rd 17 F5
Teignmouth Rd 21 F3
Templemere 7 E6
Tennyson Gdns 8 A4
Tennyson Rd 19 F3
Tensing Clo 8 A2
Tern Walk 16 D5
Testcombe Rd 23 F3
Tewkesbury Av,
  Hardway 21 G3
Tewkesbury Av, Hill Park 7 F2
Tewkesbury Clo 11 H3
Thames Dri 7 F1
Thamesmead Clo 21 F3
The Anchorage 24 A5
The Avenue, Alverstoke 23 E4
The Avenue, Fareham 7 E5
The Beachway 10 C6
The Brackens 13 F1
The Cascades 25 H2
The Causeway 9 E4
The Chantry 5 H6
The Chase, Privett 22 D2
The Chase,
  Titchfield Common 13 H1
The Chestnuts 11 F1
The Chine 20 D1
The Cloisters 7 E4
The Close, Portchester 10 B4
The Close, Titchfield 6 B6
The Coppice 17 F6
The Copse 7 F1
The Croft 15 G4
The Crossway 10 A3
The Crossways 21 G4
The Curve 16 D5
The Dell 9 E4
The Downsway 10 B4
The Drive, Fareham 8 A4

The Drive, Woodcot 16 C6
The Fairway,
The Fairway,
  Portchester 10 B4
The Fairway, Rowner 20 C1
The Firs 20 D1
The Gallops 6 A4
The Gannets 15 F5
The Gillies 8 A5
The Glade 7 F2
The Glades 5 E4
The Glebe 19 E1
The Glen 20 D1
The Greendale 7 F2
The Grove 15 F6
The Hard 25 E3
The Haven 23 F4
The Heights 8 D3
The Hillway 10 B3
The Hoe 20 D1
The Hurdles 6 A4
The Keep 10 C4
The Kingsway 10 B4
The Lane 23 F4
The Leaway 10 C4
The Leisure 17 F4
The Limes 17 F6
The Links 20 C1
The Linnets 9 F6
The Maltings 8 D3
The Mary Rose St 25 H3
The Mead 16 D5
The Meadows 8 C2
The Mews 24 C4
The Mint 20 D1
The Nook 20 D1
The Oakes 15 F4
The Paddock, Gosport 23 E2
The Paddock,
  Stubbington 15 G4
The Parade 25 E2
The Parkway 16 D6
The Pastures 5 G5
The Peregrines 9 F6
The Pines 9 G5
The Potteries 8 B3
The Precinct 24 C4
The Queens Mall 25 H4
The Queensway 10 A4
The Redan 23 G5
The Retreat 25 H6
The Ridgeway 9 E4
The Rosery 23 F4
The Scimitars 15 F5
The Seagulls 20 A6
The Shrubbery 21 F3
The Slipway 11 F5
The Spinney, Downend 9 F5
The Spinney, Rowner 20 D1
The Spur 22 D4
The Square, Elson 21 H2
The Square, Titchfield 6 C5
The Tanners 13 G2
The Thicket, Downend 9 F4
The Thicket, Holbrook 20 D1
The Timbers 7 E5
The Water 7 G1
Thetford Rd 21 E3
Thirlmere Clo 15 H4
Thomas St 25 H1
Thornbrake Rd 23 G2
Thornbury Clo 7 E5
Thorne Av 7 E2
Thorney Clo 7 F6
Thorngate Way 24 C4
Thornton Av 12 A2
Thornton Rd 21 H2
Three Tun Clo 25 F3
Tichbourne Way 20 D1
Tillingbourne 5 G6
Tintern Clo 11 E2
Tintern Rd 21 G6
Titchfield By-Pass 6 D5
Titchfield Hill 6 D5
Titchfield Park Rd 5 H6
Titchfield Rd 15 F1
Toby St 25 H2
Tollgate Rd 4 B1
Tonbridge St 25 H6
Tonnant Clo 19 E1
Tor Clo 9 E4
Toronto Pl 23 F1
Torquay Av 21 F2
Tortworth Clo 7 F5
Totland Rd 17 E6
Tower Clo 22 C3
Tower St 25 E5
Town Quay 25 E5
Trafalgar Ct 16 C1
Trafalgar Sq 21 G5
Trebourba Dri 23 E3

Trent Walk
Trent Way
Trevose Clo
Trevose Way
Triangle La
Tribe Rd
Trimaran Way 15 F5
Trinity Clo
Trinity Gdns
Trinity Grn
Trinity St
Triumph Clo
Truro Rd
Tudor Clo, Portchester
Tudor Clo, Rowner
Tudor Ct
Tukes Av
Turner Av
Turtle Clo
Twiggs End Clo
Twyford Dri
Tynedale Ct
Ulysses Ct
Ulysses Path
Unicorn Rd
Union St, Fareham
Union St, Portsmouth
Uplands Cres
Upper Brook Dri
Upper Cornaway La
Upper Old St
Upper St Michaels Gro
Upper Spinney
Upper Wharf
Vale Gro
Valentine Clo
Valley Rise
Valsheba Dri
Vanstone Rd
Vectis Rd
Ventnor Rd
Ventnor Way
Verger Clo
Vernon Clo
Vernon Rd
Veryan
Vian Clo
Vicarage La
Victoria Pl
Victoria Rd
Victoria Sq
Victoria St
Victory Rd, Portsmouth
Victory Rd, Stubbington
Vikings Clo
Village Rd
Vincent Gro
Vincent St
Vine Clo
Vineside
Violet Av
Virginia Park Rd
Vixen Clo
Vulcan Rd
Wagtail
Wakefield Av
Walford Rd
Walker Pl
Wallington Ct
Wallington Hill
Wallington Shore Rd
Wallington Way
Wallisdean Av
Walnut Dri
Walpole Rd
Waltham Clo
Waltham St
Walton Clo
Walton Ct
Walton Rd
Wandesford Pl
Warblington St
Warnford Clo
Warsash Gro
Warsash Rd
Warwick Clo
Warwick Cres
Washbrook Rd
Waterloo Rd
Waterloo St
Watersedge Rd
Waterside Gdns
Waterside La
Wavell Rd
Waveney Clo
Waverley Path
Wayfarer Clo

ESTATE PUBLICATIONS

STREET ATLASES

ASHFORD, TENTERDEN
BASILDON, BRENTWOOD
BASINGSTOKE, ANDOVER
BATH, BRADFORD ON AVON
BOURNEMOUTH, POOLE, CHRISTCHURCH
BRIGHTON, LEWES, NEWHAVEN, SEAFORD
BROMLEY (London Borough)
CHELMSFORD, BRAINTREE, MALDON, WITHAM
CHICHESTER, BOGNOR REGIS
COLCHESTER, CLACTON
CRAWLEY & MID SUSSEX
DERBY, HEANOR, CASTLE DONINGTON
EDINBURGH
EXETER, EXMOUTH
FAREHAM, GOSPORT
FOLKESTONE, DOVER, DEAL
GLOUCESTER, CHELTENHAM
GRAVESEND, DARTFORD
GUILDFORD, WOKING
HASTINGS, EASTBOURNE, HAILSHAM
HIGH WYCOMBE
I. OF WIGHT TOWNS
LEICESTER
MAIDSTONE
MANSFIELD
MEDWAY, GILLINGHAM
NEW FOREST TOWNS
NOTTINGHAM, EASTWOOD, HUCKNALL, ILKESTON
OXFORD
PLYMOUTH, IVYBRIDGE,,SALTASH, TORPOINT
PORTSMOUTH, HAVANT
READING
REIGATE, BANSTEAD, LEATHERHEAD, DORKING
RYE & ROMNEY MARSH
ST. ALBANS, WELWYN, HATFIELD
SALISBURY, AMESBURY, WILTON
SEVENOAKS
SHREWSBURY
SLOUGH, MAIDENHEAD
SOUTHAMPTON, EASTLEIGH
SOUTHEND-ON-SEA
SWALE (Sittingbourne, Faversham, I. of Sheppey)
SWINDON, CHIPPENHAM, MARLBOROUGH
TAUNTON, BRIDGWATER
TELFORD
THANET, CANTERBURY, HERNE BAY, WHITSTABLE
TORBAY
TUNBRIDGE WELLS, TONBRIDGE, CROWBOROUGH
WATFORD, HEMEL HEMPSTEAD
WEALDEN TOWNS
WEYMOUTH
WINCHESTER, NEW ALRESFORD
WORTHING, LITTLEHAMPTON, ARUNDEL

LEISURE MAPS

SOUTH EAST (1:200,000)
KENT & EAST SUSSEX (1:150,000)
SURREY & SUSSEX (1:150,000)
SOUTHERN ENGLAND (1:200,000)
ISLE OF WIGHT (1:50,000)
WESSEX (1:200,000)
DEVON & CORNWALL (1:200,000)
CORNWALL (1:180,000)
DEVON (1:200,000)
DARTMOOR & SOUTH DEVON COAST (1:100,000)
EXMOOR & NORTH DEVON COAST (1:100,000)
GREATER LONDON (1:80,000)
A DAY OUT OF LONDON (1:425,000)
EAST ANGLIA (1:250,000)
THAMES & CHILTERNS (1:200,000)
COTSWOLDS & WYEDEAN (1:200,000)
HEART OF ENGLAND (1:250,000)
WALES (1:250,000)
THE SHIRES OF MIDDLE ENGLAND (1:250,000)
SHROPSHIRE, STAFFORDSHIRE (1:200,000)
PEAK DISTRICT (1:100,000)
SNOWDONIA (1:125,000)
YORKSHIRE & HUMBERSIDE (1:250,000)
YORKSHIRE DALES (1:250,000)
NORTH YORK MOORS (1:125,000)
NORTH WEST ENGLAND (1:200,000)
ISLE OF MAN (1:60,000)
NORTH PENNINES & LAKES (1:200,000)
LAKE DISTRICT (1:75,000)
BORDERS OF ENGLAND & SCOTLAND (1:200,000)
BURNS COUNTRY (1:200,000)
ISLE OF ARRAN (1:63,360)
ARGYLL & THE ISLES (1:200,000)
HEART OF SCOTLAND (1:200,000)
GREATER GLASGOW (1:150,000)
EDINBURGH (1:150,000)
FIFE (1:100,000)
LOCH LOMOND & TROSSACHS (1:150,000)
PERTHSHIRE (1:150,000)
FORT WILLIAM, BEN NEVIS, GLEN COE (1:185,000)
IONA (1:10,000) & MULL (1:115,000)
GRAMPIAN HIGHLANDS (1:185,000)
LOCH NESS & INVERNESS (1:150,000)
AVIEMORE & SPEY VALLEY (1:150,000)
SKYE & LOCHALSH (1:130,000)
CAITHNESS & SUTHERLAND (1:185,000)
WESTERN ISLES (1:125,000)
ORKNEY & SHETLAND (1:128,000)
ENGLAND & WALES (1:650,000)
SCOTLAND (1:500,000)
HISTORIC SCOTLAND (1:500,000)
SCOTLAND CLAN MAP (1:625,000)
GREAT BRITAIN (1:1,100,000)

COUNTY ATLASES

AVON
AVON & SOMERSET
BERKSHIRE
CHESHIRE
CORNWALL
DEVON
DORSET
ESSEX
HAMPSHIRE
HAMPSHIRE (Large Format)
HERTFORDSHIRE
KENT (64pp)
KENT (128pp)
OXFORDSHIRE
SHROPSHIRE
SOMERSET
SURREY
SUSSEX (64pp)
SUSSEX (128pp)
WILTSHIRE

EUROPEAN LEISURE MAPS

EUROPE (1:3,100,000)
BENELUX (1:600,000)
FRANCE (1:1,000,000)
GERMANY (1:1,000,000)
GREECE & THE AEGEAN (1:1,000,000)
IRELAND (1:625,000)
ITALY (1:1,000,000)
MEDITERRANEAN CRUISING (1:5,000,000)
SCANDINAVIA (1:2,600,000)
SPAIN & PORTUGAL (1:1,000,000)
THE ALPS (1:1,000,000)
WORLD (1:35,000,000)
WORLD FLAT
WORLD FLAT WITH FLAGS

ESTATE PUBLICATIONS are also
sole distributors in the U.K. for:
ORDNANCE SURVEY, Republic of Ireland
ORDNANCE SURVEY, Northern Ireland

ROAD ATLAS

MOTORING IN THE SOUTH
(1:200,000)

STREET PLANS

BARNSTAPLE & ILFRACOMBE
BODMIN & WADEBRIDGE
NEWQUAY
NEWTOWN & WELSHPOOL
PENZANCE & ST IVES
ST ALBANS
TRURO
WESTON-SUPER-MARE

Catalogue and prices from ESTATE PUBLICATIONS,
Bridewell House, Tenterden, Kent TN30 6JB.
Tel: 05806 4225   Fax: 05806 3720